TEACHABLE moments

TEACHABLE
moments

BUILDING BLOCKS *of*
CHRISTIAN PARENTING

JONATHAN C. ROBINSON, PH.D.

New York

TEACHABLE moments
BUILDING BLOCKS *of* CHRISTIAN PARENTING

© 2016 JONATHAN C. ROBINSON, PH.D..

Published in New York, New York, by Morgan James Publishing. Morgan James and The Entrepreneurial Publisher are trademarks of Morgan James, LLC.
www.MorganJamesPublishing.com

The Morgan James Speakers Group can bring authors to your live event. For more information or to book an event visit The Morgan James Speakers Group at
www.TheMorganJamesSpeakersGroup.com.

A **free** eBook edition is available
with the purchase of this print book.

CLEARLY PRINT YOUR NAME ABOVE IN UPPER CASE

Instructions to claim your free eBook edition:
1. Download the BitLit app for Android or iOS
2. Write your name in **UPPER CASE** on the line
3. Use the BitLit app to submit a photo
4. Download your eBook to any device

ISBN 978-1-63047-728-8 paperback
ISBN 978-1-63047-729-5 eBook
Library of Congress Control Number:
2015913207

Cover Design by:
Rachel Lopez
www.r2cdesign.com

Interior Design by:
Bonnie Bushman
The Whole Caboodle Graphic Design

In an effort to support local communities and raise awareness and funds, Morgan James Publishing donates a percentage of all book sales for the life of each book to Habitat for Humanity Peninsula and Greater Williamsburg.

Get involved today, visit
www.MorganJamesBuilds.com

Habitat
for Humanity®
Peninsula and
Greater Williamsburg
Building Partner

Table of Contents

Author's Note

Most of us go through twelve years of grade school. Many of us go on to college, even Graduate school. We get certifications for various jobs. We get licenses to drive vehicles, to drive a forklift, to practice medicine, law, or begin other careers. Most of us, however, are parents longer than we are anything else. And yet, very few of us have any useful, organized training to be really good at this life-long job called "Parenting." Parenting is the toughest job for which most people never have any training.

As a clinical psychologist, practicing school-clinical child psychology for over thirty-five years, I have come to appreciate the value of conveying certain immutable truths about parenting. These truths, having been observed and honed in my work with over a thousand families through my clinical practice, and they apply to all families, of all backgrounds, with all sizes and permutations. These nine principles of healthy family functioning, parent-child relationship, and Godly foundation form the teachable moments of effective Christian parenting.

While families can be tossed about on the seas of specific stressors, developmental stages, sibling birth order, and family of origin experiences by both parents, the clinical wisdom of these nine principles can provide context for understanding, and ballast to right the ship and to weather all storms.

I begin this book by providing a lengthy case study. The Bower family is fictional, a patchwork of clinical cases I have treated over the years. The Bowers tell their stories, so that each family member becomes a voice, a perspective, in the healing process. No voice is predominant, more or less important, right or wrong. Each is vital, though, because they are different and unique. And they are family.

The stories become the fabric into which I weave the nine principles, thereby strengthening the cloth to resist tears and turmoil. In presenting these teachable moments, I link each principle to Scriptural truth. As we seek to find and follow God's will in our lives and in parenting our children, we build confidence, character, and commitment as parents. We provide healthy role models for our children. We accept God's direction and promise to "train your children up in the ways of the Lord, that they will not depart from it when they grow old." (Proverbs 22:6).

Finally, as an addendum, I offer appendices and Learning-the-Concept exercises that I have developed over the years. These handouts are designed to provide structure and reference to implementing the nine principles on an on-going basis in family dynamics.

I pray that God will bless you as you read this book. I pray that you find strength, hope, and foundation for your life-long journey called parenting. I hope I have reinforced all the good things you are already doing as parents and offered you valuable perspective for enhancing the lives and experience of God's most precious gift and responsibility to us—our children.

Prologue

"Fine," Jason spit at Emily, as he stomped through his bedroom door. "If you won't take me to the library to get that book, I'll just fail English Lit." He stopped and grabbed hold of the edge of the door, glaring at his sister. "And it will be your fault," Jason yelled at Emily before slamming his door shut. The door rattled against the frame as the skull and crossbones poster rustled on it. The menacing caution across the face of the poster, get out and stay out, said it all.

"Mom, wait a minute," Emily said into her cell phone, as she turned away from Jason to get more privacy. "Jason's going ballistic again."

"Well, Emily, my meeting at work ran late. I'm just calling to tell you I'll be another half hour before I get home."

Emily felt the strain in her mother's phone call. "Just hurry, Mama," she pleaded. "I'm trying to get Grace to bed, and Jason's being his usual royal pain in the you-know-where."

"Now Emily," her mother consoled, "We're all under a lot of stress." Lauren knew her eighteen year-old daughter well enough to realize that she didn't call her 'Mama' unless she had reached her limit. "I'm coming as fast as I can. Wait, that's your father."

Lauren clicked her cell phone over to the other line. "Jim, I'm so glad you called. Emily's having a crisis with the kids and I'm still a half hour away. Are you on your way home?"

"Hi, sweetheart," Jim began out of the blue. "My day was fine. Thanks for asking, and how was yours?" His sarcasm dripped from his wife's cell phone. Lauren had a habit of starting conversations in mid-stride, without the amenities Jim inherited from his Deep South upbringing.

"Jim, cut it out. Our children need us. Where are you?"

The edge in his wife's tone told Jim this was no time to make his point, again. "I'm pulling onto Sentinel Lane as we speak. Ah, there's our house up ahead, right where I left it."

"Hold on," Lauren clicked over to Emily's line.

"Sweetheart, your father is just about pulling in our driveway now. You tend to Grace. Daddy will help Jason. Hold on again," Lauren clicked back to Jim. "Thank God you're close by. I told Emily to put Grace to bed and that you would help Jason get over his meltdown."

"General ma'am, yes ma'am, *zeig heil*," Jim clicked his heels in character, as he turned into the family driveway.

"Jim, stop. I'm not feeling very playful right now. Hold on," Lauren clicked back to Emily.

"Do you see your dad outside yet?"

"Yeah, Good timing. Grace just cut herself trying to shave her legs 'like mommy and sissy do.' I gotta go."

"Emily, wait. Is she all right?"

"Just a few streaks of blood."

"Blood? Oh my God."

"Mom, it's just blood, like what we get when we don't shave that carefully either."

"But Grace is crying. I can hear her behind you. Put her on the phone."

"Mom, it's okay. I've got it covered. Let me go."

"Is your father there yet?"

"He's coming in the door just now."

"Good. Give him your cell phone and go tend to Gracie's cuts. I'm sorry I'm not there. Why is all this happening right now?"

"It's chaos central as usual. Welcome to my world, Mom." Emily handed the phone to her father, sighed, and took Gracie's little hand in hers to lead her to the bathroom.

Introduction

If this episode in the lives of the Bower family hits home to you in any way, this book and the learning series will help. How many of us live at "chaos central?" How do we restore order to chaos? What roles do faith and the example of Christ play in our finding and maintaining that order?

Lauren and Jim Bower were married nineteen years ago next month, in Lauren's home town of Colby, Georgia. They were college sweethearts. Each had grown up in the church and professed strong faith. In fact, it was their participation in Campus Crusade for Christ that had sparked the romance. Jim's quirky sense of humor and gentlemanly consideration had endeared him to Lauren, while her homespun goodness had intrigued Jim. It had all felt right. Unfortunately, the spark of romance fueled a fire of intimacy before its time, and in spite of best intentions. As soon as Lauren confirmed her suspicions, Jim "did the right thing" and they were married. Their subsequent explanation was that Emily had been "premature." But Emily really knew the truth, even if she had never made an issue of it.

At forty-two, Lauren still maintains her youthful looks. She was a knockout, blond-haired, blue-eyed, size four when Jim fell in love with her their junior year, and she still is today. Over the years, though, Jim has gotten up close and personal with Lauren's steel blue eyes, emphasis on the steel. She is as stubborn and determined as they come. Jim's pet name for her is "mini-might." Obstacles on life's path are challenges to her. She is the consummate modern woman, dual-tracked with a mid-level computer analyst career and able to maneuver around the professional speed bumps to be at every one of her children's school or athletic events. She runs a tight ship both at home and at the office. Of late, however, her home ship has sprung too many leaks for her to successfully patch up.

Easy-going Jim, on the other hand, complements his wife's drive with a roll-with-the-punches style that embraces the mantra, life's too short to get caught up in the details. When the kids were younger, he had developed his insurance business with customer presentations, cold calls, and other marketing strategies. As a full-fledged financial planner, he is now content to enjoy the residuals each year and ride the stock market with some of his high roller clients. At six foot, two inches tall, he carries a little more girth than he wants to. He rationalizes that his extra twenty pounds is the price of complacency. His work schedule is his own. He lets Lauren take the lead with church, but he is active. He's aware that he is his children's primary role model. He sees himself as the counter-balance to their mother in his children's lives. Ying and Yang.

Emily has the oldest child thing nailed down. Responsible, self-starter, good student, helpful to others. She's got her daddy's height, at five feet, ten inches tall, but her mother's looks and metabolism. Daddy keeps telling her to eat more, while mama tells him to hush, she's just fine. She's had boyfriends, but nobody serious. She's focused on finishing high school strong academically, so that she has her pick of colleges. She keeps putting off fun for later. She says she can't wait for college "so that I can finally have a life," but deep down inside, she knows she'll miss her family. In some ways, Emily has grown up too quickly, and in other ways, not at all.

Jason's the athlete his father had wanted to be. At six foot, one hundred eighty pounds, he already looks down on his big sister and postures with his dad. Jim and Jason's wrestling matches are family lore. Of late, however, Jim tries harder to win and pretends less when Jason gets the better of him. Jason might be fifteen and a high school freshman, but he acts ten most of the time, at least according to his big sister. Mom and dad, however, occasionally catch him being responsible and considerate of others. The "Keep Out!!" poster on his bedroom door is more attitude than character. He will needle Gracie and he refuses to accept that Emily's in charge in the absence of mom and dad. He wants to be left alone, as long as everybody knows it loud and clear. Mom and dad had hoped Jason would be out of the adolescent rebel stage by now, and "get it." Still feeling his way, though, Jason seems to stay on the fringe between good and evil with friends, choices, and decisions.

Grace and Emily have the "oops" factor in common. Lauren and Jim saw their family as ideal and complete after Jason was born. Then, seven years later, Gracie made a grand entrance, stage left. She even almost died at birth, having the umbilical cord wrapped around her neck not once but twice. She was anoxic. Her heart stopped briefly, and she stayed in NICU for a day as a precautionary measure. At eight years old now, Grace knows how to work the "special blessing" factor in the family. Emily and Jason see her getting away with things that they never did at her age. Mom and dad usually ignore their pleas and chalk it up to normal sibling rivalry. Grace is all girl, except when she gets that little gleam in her eye and tries to run over the soccer defender while driving for the goal.

The Bowers are surviving. They have their joys and triumphs, but also their sorrows and defeats. The children's personalities are the best and the worst of both of their parents. The developmental pulls on the parents, as well as on the children, yield conflicting goals, leading to more chaos than order in family functioning with Emily preparing to launch, and Grace now coming into her own, Jim and Lauren are keenly aware that time is growing short to make a difference in who their children grow up to become.

Jesus said that He came so that we may "have life and have it more abundantly" (John 10:10). In my over thirty-five years of clinical practice with children, adults, and families, I cite this verse repeatedly in offering the hope and goal of healing. The Bowers are surviving. Each family member, and the family as a whole, has life. No one, however, has life abundantly. Now is the time for the Bowers to step up and embrace the journey from having life to having life abundantly. It is a journey from surviving to thriving.

Healthy, vibrant families create and nurture character, responsibility, independence, and personal growth for all. Parents have succeeded in their job of parenting when they launch responsible, independent adults into the world. Weaving these teachable moments into the fabric of your family life will strengthen you on your journey from surviving to thriving and help you reach your personal and family goals. A habit is defined as any behavior that persists over time. When you want to develop a good habit, it requires consistent, repetitive effort practiced typically over four to six weeks. When you repeat a desired behavior consistently for four to six weeks, and you suddenly stop the behavior, you will miss it. It has become a new part of you.

Similarly, the journey of life often involves adapting to changing circumstances by changing your behaviors to more accurately and efficiently reach your goals. Doing so requires assessing your comfort zone and choosing to move outside your comfort zone in service to reaching your goals. Thus, we are all consistently challenged to trade in the familiar, which doesn't work as efficiently, for the unfamiliar, which has proven to work more efficiently. This is the task of forming good habits out of bad.

Contained within the text of Teachable Moments are highlighted areas entitled **Learning the Concept**. Therein is either a learning exercise or a reference to an appendix that provides you with opportunities to challenge your comfort zone, practice unfamiliar behaviors, and develop more Christ-centered parenting habits. As with all new learning, developing these tools will seem awkward and unnatural at first. With practice, however, they become second nature.

The nine teachable moments described herein provide a template for making this journey. If you and your family are surviving, but you want more, I invite you to make this journey with me.

These truths about children and teens are gleaned from my work with patients in my clinical practice. They are:

1.   Communication is relationship
2.   Clearly define who's in charge.
3.   Children will always test the limits.
4.   Children never mean what they say.

5. A family is not a democracy.
6. Hormones will wreak havoc.
7. Teenagers will rebel.
8. Problems Can Be Solved
9. Effective parents exercise the principle of responsible freedom.

Join me on this journey. Choose thriving and abundance.

Chapter One

Communication
is Relationship

I t's true in all relationships, but especially among family members. How we communicate with each other defines our relationships. Communication is the first indicator of building a relationship. The style and depth of communication tells you the level of emotional intensity and bonding being developed. Both nonverbal and verbal communication are equal partners in building healthy relationships. Conflict puts relationship under duress, and effective communication is the balm that soothes relational conflict. Active listening, the primary communication tool of healthy relationships, paves the royal road to Christ-centered parenting.

As we embark on this journey of learning how to grow kids and teens God's way, an immutable truth and the first principle of parenting is this: Communication is relationship.

Our Fully Human Example

The Christian faith accepts Jesus Christ as both fully divine and fully human. He, as God, is the *alpha and omega*. He has been from the beginning and will be with us into eternity. He, as human, provides us with an example of perfection. As we read about Jesus, the man and ministry in the Bible, we can see examples of all that is right and good with God's creation.

As Jesus chose and taught his disciples, He gave us an example of effective parenting. He laughed and played with them at the wedding at Cana (John 2:1-12). He taught them patience, tolerance, and the joy of children (Mark 10:13-16). He taught in parables, which gave his disciples opportunity to wrestle with the lessons, think for themselves, and incorporate the teachings into their daily living. When the disciples didn't get it, Jesus explained his teachings.

He dealt with sibling rivalry and was longsuffering with their shortcomings and foibles (Matt 18:1-3). When his children strayed, Jesus rebuked but did not reject (Luke 10:38-42). He even got angry. His anger, however, came in the form of righteous indignation (Matt 21:13). He held evil accountable, actions speak louder than words, but reserved judgment (Matt 12:33-37).

Jesus is our example for Christ-centered parenting and effective communication. His words conveyed his heart. His words and actions matched. He sought teachable moments with his children and spent his life building a legacy, an example for us to follow.

Building Blocks of Relationship

Communication is the first building block of relationship. I just welcomed my second grandchild into our family. We were there when our daughter gave birth. Holding a newborn in your arms is a daunting task. She is fragile. She is weak. She is dependent. She is launched into a hostile and threatening environment when birth brings her from the womb to the world. I am a part of a loving network, along with her parents and other extended family, who are charged with keeping her safe and protected, while helping her grow.

Before her birth, she listened to her mother's heartbeat. She heard her mother breathing. Now, she has suckled from her mother's breast and looked deeply into her mother's eyes. Her grip around my one little finger is sure and strong. We are communicating to her by voice, by touch, by warmth, by comfort. She is communicating to us by sight and by her cries. She has "I'm poopy" cries, "I'm hungry" cries, "I'm tired" cries, and "I hurt" cries. She also coos when she is content, and she is beginning to visually track us in her surroundings. We are communicating to each other. We are building relationship.

The style and depth of communication is indicative of a developing emotional intensity and bonding experience. A famous research study and its follow-up in mother-child bonding(Harlow, 1958; Jeddi, 1970) let a rhesus monkey spend time with either a cloth covered monkey mannequin or a wire-meshed monkey mannequin. The young monkey instinctively and repeatedly chose to spend time with the cloth covered mannequin. This seminal work defined the concept of "contact comfort" in bonding and building parent-child relationships.

Even though Skype computer technology gives children opportunity to see and talk to their parent via computer link when the parent is off to war or away on extended business trips, such long distance relationship never takes the place of being there for your child as much as you can. Proximity increases the depth of communication.

The intent and content of communication defines your style in building healthy relationships with your child and family. Emotional intensity and bonding experiences are developed as you vary time and opportunity to be with your child. In addition to Directional Communication, that helps our children be safe, and Instructional Communication, that helps them learn and grow, parents more often overlook opportunities to have Check-In Time with their children. Finally, as a Christ-centered parent, you want to be ever vigilant to spot Teachable Moments when interacting with your child.

Saturday Morning at the Bowers

After handling the crises of Friday evening, with Emily helping her sister, Grace, clean up from her cuts and go to bed, while Jim collared his son, Jason, to help him settle down and get his schoolwork needs met, the Bowers all went to bed and then woke up Saturday morning. This was usually their most leisurely morning of the week and they had made a habit of having a family breakfast. It was one of the few mornings in the week the kids could enjoy their dad's famous "the works" omelet or their mom's scratch pancakes smothered in syrup. Some got up early, others later, but all made a point to be at the table for a 10 AM breakfast with hungry appetites in hand. Jim and Lauren sat by the ends of the breakfast table after serving the family. Emily sat to her dad's left and beside Grace, while Jason slouched in his chair opposite his sisters.

"Mm mm, Mama, these pancakes… are… delicious." Emily raved between mouthfuls.

"Hey, no fair," Grace chimed in. "I want some too. Pass those babies this way," she directed her father. She reached toward her dad to snag a pancake off the serving plate.

"Now Grace. Settle down," her dad cautioned. "You'll get your pancakes when it's your turn." He turned to his son and continued, "Jason, pick your pleasure. Pancakes or omelet for you this morning?"

Jason grumbled and began to uncoil from his slouch. His mom wanted to correct her son's table manners, but decided to hold off for now.

"What's this stuff in the omelet?" Jason groused.

"That's peppers. Pieces of red peppers and green peppers, you know, to give the omelet a festive look and to perk up the flavor."

"Yuck." Jason glided back into his slouch.

"Okay, then," his dad continued undaunted, "pick the pancakes this morning." He started to slide the spatula under two pancakes on the serving platter and transfer them to his son's plate.

"Dad, why do you have to be so upbeat? It's still the middle of the night."

Jason's mom chimed in, "Don't be such a grump, Son." His dad finished transferring the pancakes and smiled, without comment.

"Grump. Grump. Grumpy grump." Grace sing-songed across the table. "My turn for pancakes, Pop." Jim turned to serve Grace.

"Grump this, you twerp," Jason barked at his little sister. "I was up until 3 AM last night trying to get to the top level on my computer game, but I kept getting outsmarted by the enemy. So leave me alone."

"Yeah." Jim noted, sneaking in a teachable moment, "The enemy will outsmart us at every turn if we let him. We can't take him on alone."

"What are you talking about?" Jason blurted out of his fog.

"3 AM, huh? His mom added, "and yet you knew that breakfast would be at 10 AM regardless. Hmmm." She paused for effect and concluded, "no wonder you're tired, but, you know, Jason, that still doesn't give you the right to bark at your sister."

"Yeah." Grace added, and then stuck her tongue out.

"I think you owe Grace an apology, Son," Lauren directed before cutting her eyes at Grace.

"Sorry." Jason spit through gritted teeth.

"And, Grace," Lauren continued, turning toward her younger daughter, "I think you owe your brother an apology for teasing and baiting him."

Grace looked dumbstruck. She sputtered, "but...but..."

"Grace...? " Jim concurred with his wife.

"Okay, fine. Sorry, Jason," she offered an unfelt apology.

The Bower family ate in stunted silence for a while before Jim changed direction. "Well, that was fun." Nobody laughed or even looked up. "So, let's talk about plans for the day."

Each family member spoke in turn about their expectations for the day. Jim and Lauren encouraged the discussion and asked questions about how their plans could be accommodated and coordinated. Each then carried their dishes to the sink, rinsed them, and put them in the dishwasher. The morning was off and running.

Directional, Instructional, Check-In, and Teachable Moments

This little slice of the Bowers' Saturday morning is offered to illustrate several points. First, family communication is never easy or smooth. Family moments of moods, attitudes, and expectations all aligning in perfect synchrony are rare. They are the picture of "life doesn't get any better than this." This vignette is more the norm than the exception. Second, the depth and variation of communication in relationship is constantly changing. As parents, we are to be aware of those constant changes, adapt accordingly, and hold on for dear life. The four levels of communication in families can be present in ever-changing fashion. As parents, we are to take advantage of opportunities to direct, instruct, check in, and teach each and all of our children.

Offering direction to our children comes most easily to us. Of course we want them to be safe. The younger they are, the more direction they require. When Jim told Grace to "settle down, you'll get your pancakes when it's your turn," he was both directing and instructing. The meaning within his words reinforced that families take turns and are patient. Direction and instruction are the most conflict-free components of healthy family communication.

When Jim explained to Jason what those "red and green things" were in the omelet, he offered instruction. Instruction is a natural use of the parent as the resident expert on matters. Young children hunger for instruction and will often come to the parent for help. Teens, on the other hand, are not as easy to instruct. When you bump up against attitude from your teen (or youngster for that matter), ask permission before you instruct. For example, a mom might see her young teen struggling with make-up and ask, "You know, I'm a regular make-up whiz. Can I offer some pointers?" If your child declines your help, respect her wishes and add, "maybe later," or, "Well, if I can ever be of help, let me know, okay?" In this way, you are leaving the door open for her to come to you later.

Check-in communication gives you opportunity to keep current in your child's life. The Bowers' Saturday morning breakfast ritual provides them with a context within which to check in with each child. After the meal is ideal, in that, hopefully, the children are sated, comfortable, and more likely to comply. Check-ins are questions designed to find out "what's up" with your child. In addition to daily events and expectations, questions like, "How's that lit project coming?" and, "Do you have the clothes you need for tomorrow?" are check-in moments.

In addition to finding out plans for upcoming events, check-ins also include what I call the "How was your day, dear?" time. In essence, this is a debriefing on events of the day. You can follow up on morning expectations, as well as give your child opportunity to talk about anything that is on his mind related to how his day went. Check-ins keep all relationships current and vital. Healthy marriages make a habit of checking in with each other frequently as well.

When my son was a teenager, we would banter over check-ins. Often, it would go like this:

"Hey, son. What's up?"

"Nothing."

"How was school today?"

"Fine."

"What did you learn about today?"

"Stuff."

"What kind of stuff?"

"You know, stuff stuff."

"Was it mostly yellow stuff, or oblique stuff?"

"Okay, Dad, now you're weird."

Although sometimes that was the extent of our conversation, I tried and he responded. We connected. The hidden message in check-ins is that we care.

Teachable moments are the lifeblood of effective parenting. Christ-centered parents are always on the lookout for them. We even sneak them into the conversation, as Jim did when he commented on Jason's difficulty getting past the bad guys on his computer game to succeed to the next level. More often, though, teachable moments are crafted from our experiences. They, too, are usually better received by asking permission before launching into your mini-lesson.

If Emily were to come home from a bad date and her mom caught her before she tumbled into bed, she might bend her mom's ear for a while about her date. Lauren could seize the teachable moment with a summary comment like, "Sweetheart, I'm so sorry you suffered through this date with a jerk. It sounds like a wasted evening. Some guys just don't get it and stay in jerk mode. Thankfully, all guys are not jerks. Hang in there. God has Mr. Right for you somewhere out there."

Such teachable moments are outside of the classroom, have no reading assignments and no discernible exam. They happen in life, in real time, and they have immediate and lasting impact. The outcome is less important than the process. You may not be able to relate to what your child is experiencing and you may not have the right answer for her. You are, however, there for her. Your efforts to help provide the emotional bonding of the teachable moment.

Learning the Concept: Exercise 1, Types of Communication

Four types of basic communication apply in parent-child relationships. When you are telling your child what to do, you are using **Directional Communication (DC).** When you are giving your child information that will help broaden their knowledge base and help them learn, you are using **Instructional Communication (IC).** When you want to connect with them in the moment, you are defining **Check-In Time (CI).** When you have your child's full attention to give him some of your wisdom with the intent and context in which to use it, you have defined a **Teachable Moment (TM).**

Beside each of the items listed below, mark DC, if the item is an example of Direct Communication. Mark IC if the item is an example of Instructional Communication. If the item conveys an opportunity for you to Check-In with your child, mark it CI. If you see the beginnings of a Teachable Moment with your child, mark TM.

1. _____ Be careful, Sweetheart. Don't go too close to the water. It's way over your head.

2. _____ Dude, what's up?

3. _____ Okay, now, put the worm on your hook like this, so it won't wiggle off.

4. _____ Boy, when I was your age, my dad used to tear up my butt for the least little thing. Now, I don't do that with you. Do you want to know why?

5. _____ Rise and shine, big guy. We've got work to do.

6. _____ Here, Sugar. Let me help you tie that shoe.

7. _____ Hey, Darlin'. How was your day?

8. _____ What makes you think you're ready to learn how to drive?

9. _____ You know, sharing works really good. First, when you share, you make a friend. Also, sharing helps you enjoy giving, instead of just getting all the time.

10. _____ When you want to make a good choice, write down all the pros and cons, and then go with the longer list.

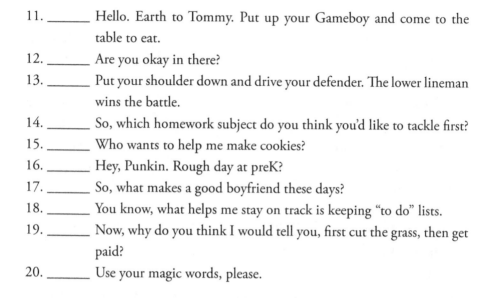

11. _____ Hello. Earth to Tommy. Put up your Gameboy and come to the table to eat.

12. _____ Are you okay in there?

13. _____ Put your shoulder down and drive your defender. The lower lineman wins the battle.

14. _____ So, which homework subject do you think you'd like to tackle first?

15. _____ Who wants to help me make cookies?

16. _____ Hey, Punkin. Rough day at preK?

17. _____ So, what makes a good boyfriend these days?

18. _____ You know, what helps me stay on track is keeping "to do" lists.

19. _____ Now, why do you think I would tell you, first cut the grass, then get paid?

20. _____ Use your magic words, please.

Verbal and Nonverbal Communication

Verbal communication in relationship building gets all the press. Nonverbal communication is often seen merely as the backdrop for verbal communication. However, each is vital and instrumental in creating emotionally healthy relationships. With children and teens especially, facial expressions, posture, gait, breath, and gaze all convey meaningful nonverbal communication. If you only zoom in on his words, you will miss vital information to help decode what your son is trying to say.

Nonverbal communication also is a portal into deeper feeling. Later in this book I will explain why children never mean what they say. As parents, it's up to us to decode their words. Tuning into their nonverbal language gives us the tools we need to decode. Perceptive parents will find themselves noticing disparity between your child's words and actions. "I hear what you are saying, but your actions don't match your words. What else is going on?" A shuffling gait can mean "I don't want to go." An eye roll or shoulder shrug can mean "Leave me alone." A vacant gaze can mean "All I hear right now is blah, blah, blah. I'm not getting it, or I don't want to."

As parents, we have our own arsenal of nonverbal communication as well. When I was growing up, I remember my dad as kind, gentle, and ever patient with me. However, when I crossed the line, he never said a word. He never got mad at me. He gave me "THE LOOK." His look of disappointment melted away all of my resolve to take him on. I quickly conformed to his expectations.

I often tell parents that kids are the emotional barometer of what's going on in the family. They know what we are feeling long before we know. Children will take parent nonverbal cues and respond accordingly. As both children and parents develop awareness of and congruity between both our nonverbal and verbal communication, emotionally healthy family relationships bloom.

Learning the Concept: Exercise 2, Verbal and Non-Verbal Communication, What Does It Mean?

The tuning in and decoding process of communication often sets the tone for how effectively we communicate with our children. Helping our children avoid mixed messages and clarifying their intent and meaning increases the emotional intensity and bonding of our relationships.

Below are verbal and nonverbal descriptors in the left hand column and possible meanings in the right hand column. Match the columns by putting the letter of the decoded meaning in the space beside the number of the descriptor. After matching the meaning to the descriptor, mark whether the match is **Verbal (V)**, **Nonverbal (NV)**, or **Both (B)** and whether the message is **Clear (C)** or **Mixed (M)**.

1. _____ Come here this very minute, young man.

A. I heard your question, and I know I should but I don't really want to listen right now

2. _____ Blank stare from your child after you ask her a question.

B. Disappointed and/or angry. I will get to the bottom of this.

3. _____ Sitting on the ground, holding her knee, and sniffling softly.

C. I know I should want you to go, but I don't

4. _____ Long, lingering, tight hug.

D. Loving the attention, even if it's negative and/or mad.

5. _____ OK Dad, in a minute.

E. I don't know what the right thing is to say. I am scared and/or mad.

6. _____ The Look!

F. I'm loving it.

7. _____ Daughter busting a move while listening to her IPod.

G. I'm serious and need your input.

8. _____ Sure, Son. What's on your mind? (while reading the newspaper.)

H. Finally. Exuberance. Victory.

9. _____ Have a good time (said with a shaky voice and through gritted teeth).

I. I didn't hear you and don't want to hear you.

10. _____ Son, we need to talk. Come sit with me (patting the couch cushion beside you).

J. I'm angry and/or disappointed. You didn't just do that.

11. _____ I don't like peas. Clenched teeth, tight lipped.

K. Look at how different and unique I am.

12. _____ Joey's teasing me and won't leave me alone (said running and giggling).

L. I'm in control and digging in my heels.

13. _____ Staring at TV and no response to a direction or question.

M. If I put you off, maybe you'll forget or do it yourself.

14. _____ Checkmate! Hah! (Hands thrust over his head.)

N. I love you so much.

15. _____ Outlandish, multi colored jeans, bling and piercings, T-shirt stating, "don't look at me."

O. I'm trying to be brave, but it hurts.

16. _____ Arms crossed over chest, scowling, chair turned completely around.

P. I don't want to stop playing.

17. _____ (Running past you in tears) I'm never going to school ever again!

Q. I did what you wanted.

18. _____ I said I'm sorry. Now leave me alone.

19. _____ If you can't get anybody else, I'll help.

20. _____ (Legs crossed, bouncing on tip toes) No, Mama, I don't have to pee.

R. I won't let you down, even if I want to.

S. I may have to be here, but I'm not talking.

T. I'm soooo embarrassed.

When Conflict Erupts—Active Listening

Consider normal, healthy family communication to be similar to your child having no fever. His emotional temperature is 98.6 degrees. There's laughter, give and take, and cooperation. Chores are getting finished without hassle. Kids are playing nicely together. There's banter, questions, answers, direction, check-ins, and teachable moments.

Now, consider when your child has a problem. If it were a cold or the flu, his temperature would go up. He would be sniffly, sneazy, with aches and pains, nausea, maybe vomiting. His body is trying to deal with and ward off infection. His symptoms are the body's way of doing this. The higher the fever, the more infection and illness you have to treat. He needs medicine and time to heal.

When your child is in emotional or relational conflict, his words and actions tell you just how high his emotional fever is climbing. He needs soothing words of understanding, empathy, to help bring his emotional fever down. Just as you keep alert for physical symptoms of illness, so too do you need to put your radar up to catch the words and actions of your child that define emotional distress and relational conflict.

Active listening paves the royal road to relationship in Christ-centered families. Active listening leads to your child feeling heard, feeling your empathy for his conflict. It is the primary communication tool to calm conflict in the family. It precedes substantive, positive change in family interactions. It soothes the savage beasts of defiance, rage, and disrespect. With timely application, it minimizes outbursts and precedes helping children redirect their energies in more productive ways.

Fundamentally, active listening is your effort to stay tuned into your child's feelings in a timely fashion. Its basic format is simple, "You feel…" The variations on this format are abundant. Additionally, the communication tools of passive listening, parroting, paraphrasing, and noncommittal response (See Appendix 1) are variations on the theme of tuning into your child's feelings. The more creative you are in active listening, the more likely you are to get and keep your child's attention. He will only cooperate freely in addressing his concerns after he feels heard and understood. Active listening affords your child the best and fastest means of feeling heard and understood.

As Appendix 1 describes, active listening requires your full and total attention on your child's perspective of his conflict. You may disagree with his behavior, You may not remotely imagine how he could feel the way he does. You may have the perfect solution to his problem. None of that matters until and unless he feels heard and understood. When your child is in conflict, your active listening what he has to say is your best way to reduce his "fever," that is, to lower the intensity of what he is feeling.

The Way the Cookie Crumbles

Grace saw Jason come out of the kitchen one night with several chocolate chip cookies from the porcelain kitty cat cookie jar that sat atop the kitchen counter. He went into the den and flopped down on the Laz-e-Boy recliner to watch his TV shows. Those cookies looked really good to her, and so she bounced off the couch and trotted into the kitchen to get a handful for herself. Lauren heard her daughter stomp out of the kitchen moments later and into the den. Jason was dead meat.

"Why do you have to always be such a big jerk? You could have left some cookies for somebody else, you know." She stood next to her big brother by the side of the recliner. Jason barely even looked up at Gracie.

"You snooze, you lose, you little bug," Jason blinked and turned back to watching his show. "You should have gotten there before me if you wanted some cookies," he added. "Mmm, they are really good."

Gracie stomped her feet and reached out to grab a cookie out of Jason's hand. As she had heard the voices of her children get louder and more heated,

Lauren got up from her desk in the kitchen alcove and hustled into the den. She got between her flailing children and pulled Grace back.

"Lemme go," Gracie fumed, "I'm gonna make Jason pay for being such a jerk."

Lauren picked up her little girl, Gracie's arms and legs still flailing, and hauled her out of the den. She took her to the living room and sat her down on the couch. Lauren sat down beside her daughter, who was about to melt into tears. She pulled Gracie to her and hugged her tightly.

"Oh, Baby, I'm so sorry. You really wanted some of those cookies, didn't you?"

"He's always doing this kind of stuff. You know the world is not only about Jason and what he wants," Gracie protested.

"He was being selfish. He hurt your feelings."

"Yeah," Gracie forced out the word between sobs. "It's not fair."

"No, Sweetie, it's not. You didn't get to the cookies first. You are the youngest and smallest in the family. And if you had gotten to the cookies, you would have left a few for others or even offered some to Jason, knowing how much he likes chocolate chip cookies, like you do."

"I'm never giving him another cookie. Never ever."

"You want your brother to hurt like you do right now, huh? You feel hurt and powerless. Those are crumby feelings, aren't they?"

After more discussion between them, Gracie's tears dried up and she and her mom made a date to bake more cookies together tomorrow morning, any kind that Gracie wanted. Lauren made a mental note to confront Jason later about his attitude toward his little sister.

If this little vignette seems too perfect and surreal, that's because it is. I'm giving you an ideal example, an idea of the power of active listening at its best. How many of us, even the most well intentioned among us parents, would have come to Gracie's rescue. I would have fought the urge to declare, "Stop it, you two. Jason, in this family we share. How could you so thoughtlessly empty the cookie jar? Grace, settle down. I'll handle this. Jason, give me all of your remaining cookies and go to your room. You're grounded for the rest of the night." After all, as parents we are primarily peacekeepers, aren't we?

Well, no, peacekeeping is only a minor part of the parent job description. It's not even necessary if we are really good at relationship building. While my little rant would have saved Gracie, it also would have alienated Jason more than he already was. Gracie would surely have beamed a smug smile to Jason as he huffed up the stairs. The next skirmish in the sibling wars would have quite naturally been just around the bend.

Learning the Concept: Exercise 3, Feeling Words and Sharing Feelings

Using Appendix 2 as a "cheat sheet," talk to one another about your feelings. You can use this list of feelings in a variety of ways. Share with each other five feelings you love to have, five feelings you hate to have, five feelings you've never had, five feeling words you don't understand, and so forth. Describe situations or circumstances in which you experienced these feelings. Whoever is listening at the time, be aware of active listening, as this will help draw out the speaker's feelings.

If there is a core, universal, rapport-building, communication tool, active listening is it. Parents who actively listen to their children are allowed inside the child's world. They open their child to an understanding of what they are feeling, of which oftentimes the child is unaware. They unlock understanding, emotional intimacy, and a closer relationship.

However, active listening does not come naturally to many parents. Our need to be in power, to maintain control and discipline, to solve problems, and to know-it-all gets in the way of our using active listening effectively. This communication skill takes time and practice to master.

Active Listening Do's and Don't's

After reviewing Appendices 1, 2, and 3, you will get more comfortable with the words and intent of active listening. However, what you don't do is equally important to what you do when active listening. First, don't solve the problem for your child. While potentially effective in the short run and time efficient, your hidden message to your child is this, "You really are so dumb, immature, and incompetent that I need to solve this one for you. Get out of my way." No parent would ever willingly, knowingly, say these words to your child in need, but that's the hidden message of taking over the child's problem without permission and solving it for her.

Second, don't judge, criticize, or rebuke your child in need or in conflict. Lauren could have told Gracie, "Honey, you should know better than to expect Jason to save a cookie for you. What were you thinking?" This response shifts your focus from her feelings to her behavior. She gets no benefit from such a response, and she would likely feel shamed.

Third, don't minimize your child's upset, or make it about you. Lauren could have told her daughter, "It's just a cookie, and no big deal. And besides, your uncle Joey made my life miserable when we were growing up. Now look at him. He's nice as he can be. So, it's all good in the end." Such a well-intentioned comment would only have contributed to Gracie feeling small, insecure, and insignificant.

As you active listen, you can actually feel your child's emotional temperature go down. When you think she is calmed down sufficiently, then join her in problem-solving her conflict. Such comments as, "Well, now that you seem calmer, what can you do to avoid this conflict in the future?" If you have suggestions, preface your counsel with getting your child's permission, such as, "Hey, I've got some ideas. Wanna hear them?"

Appendix 1 provides you with a handout that will walk you through the development of active listening skills. This **Listening/Sharing Exercise** can be used by all family members. The more skilled you are at identifying feelings (yours and others), the more freedom you have to effect positive change. **Appendices 2 and 3** go together. Couples are asked at first to use the feelings word list to find three positive feelings from your distant past, before you even met or knew each other. In sharing those feelings and circumstances with your spouse, the spouse is freed to practice active listening with total objectivity.

As the Listening/Sharing Exercise is practiced repeatedly, couples can move toward more contemporary experiences and more inflammatory circumstances. This is harder active listening and requires a taking turns approach, but it is an excellent tool for mature, loving couples to use as a prelude to creative problem-solving.

While the exercise itself is quite structured, with practice you can remove the time constraints and use the active listening skills when anyone in your family comes to you with a problem or concern. Frequently, I ask couples to use this exercise as a lead-in to what I call their "How Was Your Day, Dear" time. This is fifteen minutes or so apart from distractions where you can check in with each other. It would also apply where you want to see how your child's day was as well.

Learning the Concept: Exercise 4, Active Listening and Its Variations

As a way to "get" your child, there is no better resource than active listening. Along with its variations, your message to your child is clear: I want to understand what you are feeling. I support your abilities to figure out how to feel better. Farthest from active listening is **Passive Listening (PL)**. You are attentive, looking at your child, and listening fully, but not talking at all. Passive Listening is also known as silence. An active way of telling your child that you are listening, but without interrupting or interjecting, is to make a **Non-Committal Response (NCR)**. These comments are words of encouragement for your child to continue to talk ("Go on."), exclamations ("Really? Wow!"), or merely space fillers ("Uh huh."). Closer to active listening, for purposes of clarifying what you are hearing, you can **Parrot (PT)** your child's comments. This is a word-for-word playback, so that he can hear what he just said to you. It leaves no room for misinterpretation or misunderstanding. However, even with heartfelt intent, if done to excess, parroting can become annoying. Closer still is **Paraphrasing (PR)**, where you are trying to understand the context of your child's comments. This is helpful in providing your child with different perspectives on the topic, but does not help him expand his awareness of his feelings. When you **Active Listen (AL)** your child, you help him expand the feeling possibilities, more broadly incorporating his feelings and context. Your message is, "I hear you. I understand."

For each of the items below, mark to the left of the item either PL, NCR, PT, PR, or AL, based on whether you think the item reflects passive listening, a noncommittal response, parroting, paraphrasing, or active listening.

1. _____ What you said was, you don't get it.
2. _____ So you might be feeling taken advantage of.
3. _____ Oh no!
4. _____ You want me to drive you to your friend's house.
5. _____ I'm sorry, baby. That looks like it really hurts.
6. _____ Uh huh.
7. _____ What else happened?
8. _____ You're stuck.
9. _____ I understand you don't want to come in for dinner, however, it's dinner time.
10. _____ Hmmm
11. _____ It must feel so surreal to you right now.
12. _____ So, I guess you think people don't play by the rules much, huh.
13. _____ You don't have any money.
14. _____ I wonder if what you are saying is only part of the story.
15. _____ You're stuck?
16. _____ What a mess.
17. _____ You mean you have nothing to wear.
18. _____ It's so sad when a boy breaks up with you.
19. _____ You're spitting nails mad and you don't know what to do with it.
20. _____ Leaning forward slightly in your chair, looking intently at her.
21. _____ Stopping what you are doing to give him your undivided attention.
22. _____ You're not sure where you want to go with this decision.
23. _____ You need more time?
24. _____ Oh, brother. For real? Tell me more.
25. _____ So, you know what to do, but not how to do it.

SUMMARY

We communicate in our families from the moment of conception. Life is communicating. Communication is relationship. Whether it is nonverbal or verbal, whether if involves directing, instructing, checking in, or finding teachable moments, you will have healthier relationships in your family with the more effort you put into effective communication with each and every family member.

Jesus Christ provides us the example of effective communication. He embraced all of his feelings and shared those feelings with his flock. Christ-centered parenting starts with taking Jesus' lead.

All families will have conflict. Active listening is the communication tool that best addresses conflict. Active listening focuses on the relationship and the process rather than on the outcome. It empowers children to address and effectively deal with their conflicts. As we practice active listening within our families, we nurture our children to grow in God's way.

Lord, You are the Way, the Truth, and the Light. Shine through me and onto my family. Help me to direct my family in Your ways. Help me to be aware of teachable moments and to empower my children to settle their own conflicts. Help me to communicate effectively and to lead by example. Thank you, Lord, for your grace, your wisdom, and your example. Amen.

Chapter Two

Who's in Charge?

This seems like a rather innocuous question. Of course the dad's in charge. Of course God's in charge, isn't He? If everything is so obvious, then why is authority such a bone of contention in many families? Even the concept of authority is confusing. There is ascribed authority and earned authority. Ascribed authority comes with the job title. "Dad" means "in charge." Ascribed authority. The authority comes from the role. And yet, there are times, many times, when dad is not there to be in charge.

With over 60% of American homes requiring two family incomes, according to the last U.S. census, mom is there only slightly more than dad. Many teenagers grow up as "latch key kids," where they are home alone, or home tending to younger siblings, for up to three hours before either parent gets home from work. If the title "Dad" floats through the family according to availability, then who's really in charge? If the family is churched, but mom is more active, more openly spiritual than dad, where is God in the mix of family dynamics? Of course God's in charge, but is He?

And then there is earned authority, which can add to the confusion. Earned authority does not come with the job title. It is inherent in the interactions of the individual. When someone is available, shows initiative, is compassionate and understanding of all parties involved in all facets of the problem, and leads by example, then that person develops earned authority. It is developed over time, as trust, confidence, and a positive track record increase. When that person also has the title, earned and ascribed authority merge, creating the best of both worlds. When one person in a family has the title, but another has earned the authority, increased family conflict is likely. When all family members are vying for authority, welcome to chaos central.

Earned Authority vs. Ascribed Authority—Case Example

In the Bower family, Lauren is well-intentioned but overwhelmed. She's driving home from work with a million things on her mind. Did that data entry staffer really understand what she was trying to tell him? Is the project manager going to like the changes she has suggested to her department's software? How could she let work spill over onto her home and hearth again? Is she asking too much of Emily? Lauren takes charge by calling ahead as she is coming home, both to check on things and to let her daughter know that she is thinking about her, but also to assert her authority, take control, be in charge.

Jim, on the other hand, has a different leadership style. He tries to be the calm in the storm. He chose less frenetic work that allows him to float, encourage, and be involved without having to be in charge. Even though Lauren gives out the orders over the phone, it's likely that Jim would have calmed the Jason storm when he got home anyway, while also affirming and encouraging Emily to take care of Gracie's boo-boos.

Emily is the default authority in her parents' absence. As the oldest child, and with some maturity, she has grown into the role over time. She may not know any other way to be around her younger siblings, thus potentially creating conflict and confusion when one or both of her parents are at home. While the role is natural, even enjoyable for Emily, it may deprive her of her own growing up experiences. Her mom and dad will want to help her safeguard "Emily time," where she gets to hang out with her friends, enjoy her own hobbies and activities, and grow in her individuality. If she feels that she is "just the babysitter" in the family, then she will find her own form of adolescent rebellion, rife with resentment and contention. Those in default authority often have the least influence over others.

Jason and Grace are in their own worlds. Neither wants to be in charge in the family, but each wants attention in their own ways. Each is developmentally dependent on others for need gratification. When untended, each will find a way to draw attention from whomever is in charge. They are in positions to try to force their will on others around them. At chaos central both Jason and Grace have entered the fray with Emily and their parents, Lauren and Jim, to define who's in charge.

Healthy Families

Healthy families can look to Scripture and to Jesus' example to define and exercise leadership. The Bible starts with a clear understanding of what God wants:

> "So God created humans to be like himself; he made men and women. God gave them his blessing and said, 'Have a lot of children! Fill the earth with people and bring it under your control.'" (Genesis 1:27-28, Contemporary English translation)

God wants us to have children, raise them by His example, and be in control of them. In our politically correct and overpopulated world, "have children" could be extrapolated to include raising children other than biologically our own, such as extended family children, foster children, adopted children, lost children. Solomon added the core mandate of parenting:

> "Raise your children up in the ways of the Lord, that they will not depart from it." (Proverbs 22:6)

As parents, our sources are God's Will and His Word. I like this translation because men and women have parity. We are all of God. We are to jointly raise our children and be in authority over them. But is it to be earned or ascribed authority? The answer is both. God gave us this gift, blessing, and responsibility. Therefore our authority is ascribed from God. How we use that authority determines whether it is a blessing or a curse, whether there is calm, purposeful interaction in the family or there is chaos.

In the Bower family, the chaos is fomented by blurred boundaries, questions about who is in charge and what is expected of each person. When I see a family for counseling and the child is wreaking havoc in my office, I know who's in charge. Parents are in charge when they convey authority, set firm boundaries, and work with their children on meeting their needs within those boundaries. For the Bowers, Lauren wanted to be in charge, Jason was challenging that, Jim wanted to help, and Emily was trying to survive the chaos until the cavalry arrived. Lauren felt the situation spiraling out of control because she was trying to parent on the fly. She got flustered by having to adjust her thinking when her work meeting ran late.

While both ascribed and earned authorities are critical for healthy family functioning, all parties are more cooperative when earned authority takes precedence. When the emphasis of ascribed authority is control at all cost, children and spouses will rebel. "Because I said so," is the worst rationale for parents in directing their children. They are left dangling and defiant.

Older generations today bemoan the fact that today's children don't fear adults. Fear is never a good foundation for healthy parenting. When we accept God's will to have children as a gift, a blessing, and a responsibility, then we have little need to control them by acting in ways that cause them to fear us.

In his letter to the church at Ephesus, the apostle Paul puts the healthy parent-child relationship in perspective:

"Children, you belong to the Lord, and you do the right thing when you obey your parents. The first commandment with a promise says, 'Obey your father and your mother, and you will have a long and happy life.' Parents, don't be hard on your children. Raise them properly. Teach them and instruct them about the Lord." (Ephesians 6:1-4)

Learning the Concept: Exercise 5, Earned Authority vs. Ascribed Authority

Parents who are able to develop an earned authority with their children have more credibility in their guidance and decision-making. Children will listen to you because they know you have their best interests at heart. They know you are partnering with them in the process of their growing up. This is a "softer, gentler" kind of parental authority. The focus is on cooperation and relationship

Ascribed authority, on the other hand, is all about control and outcome. Parents have ascribed authority because you are the parent. You are in charge. What you say goes. Parents who exercise earned authority are in control as well. The difference usually is in context and delivery. How you say it is as important as what you say. The fewer words you use in explaining or directing your child, the greater likelihood you are exercising ascribed authority.

Look at the following quotes from parents as they explain or direct their children. Put an **E** on the space to the left of the comment for those items you see as representative of **Earned Authority** Put an **A** on the space to the left of the comment for those items you see as representative of **Ascribed Authority**

1. _____ Come on, sweetheart. It's time to get up.
2. _____ Help me take the trash out, please.
3. _____ Do it now.
4. _____ Let's tackle that homework after dinner.
5. _____ Because I said so.
6. _____ You're working so hard. Why don't you take a break, and we'll get back to it in twenty minutes.
7. _____ You have got ten minutes to finish that up, buster, or you're in trouble.
8. _____ What's wrong with you?
9. _____ Gosh, you're taking longer than I thought. Is there a problem? How can I help?
10. _____ Okay. That's it. Get over here.

11. _____ Let's go, Bucko. Get outta bed now.
12. _____ Now, sloooowly turn left. Slowly. I said, slowly. Too fast! Yaaah. We're gonna die.
13. _____ It's okay, sweetheart, let it all out. Guys can be such jerks sometimes.
14. _____ I said ten minutes for your shower. It's been twelve minutes now. Out, young man.
15. _____ Forget about hanging with your friends for now. You're helping me rake the leaves.
16. _____ I know you want to hang with your friends, but do you mind helping me rake these leaves for a while? I would really appreciate it.
17. _____ Where are your manners, mister?
18. _____ Here's the job jar. Who wants to pick first? Let's go. The sooner we get to it, the faster it will all get done.
19. _____ Everybody gets to do something, even you, peanut.
20. _____ What part of "no" did you not understand?

Servanthood Parenting

God sent parents to children to be His emissaries. God sent Jesus to be parents' role model. Jesus' parenting of his flock is the ideal role model for our parenting of our children. Through his ministry and example, he gained an earned authority to parent his followers. He preached servanthood when he explained that "the last shall be first and the first shall be last" (Matthew 19: 30). When explaining his ministry, he told us to feed him, clothe him, visit him in jail. The disciples did not understand, and Jesus followed with, "when you do these things to the least of you, you do them to me" (Matthew 25:40).

When he stripped down to his loin cloth before the Last Supper, knelt before each disciple and washed and dried their feet, Peter was horrified. Peter protested that his master would never bend so low before him. Jesus admonished that, unless he would follow his example of servanthood, he would never be a leader.

Through our servanthood as parents, we develop earned authority. Our children follow our direction because they want to, not only because they have to. We lead by example. Serving our children does not mean they are in charge. Many children today suffer from an entitlement expectation, where their privileges are taken for granted, seen as rights to which they are entitled. When parents use their earned authority and model servant leadership, they do not give in to the child's every whim. Rather, the balance of reward and consequence from parents keeps children on the right path. We serve our children by responding to their needs, looking ahead to the bigger picture, equipping them for becoming responsible adults.

Learning the Concept: Exercise 6, Servanthood Parenting

Are "servanthood" and "parenting" two words that actually go together? Can you be a servant to your kids and have any authority as their parent? The answer to both questions is a resounding yes. As Jesus led by serving, so too does he want us to parent by serving our children. Serving and being a servant are distinctly different. As a servant, you do whatever your child wants, and when he wants it. The child is in charge. This is never a good idea. By serving, you role model for your child how healthy relationships work, how to be helpful, and how Jesus wants us to be. Children want to cooperate and abide by house rules and parental expectations when you exercise earned authority through the practice of servanthood parenting.

Look at the following quotes and decide whether each one indicates you are being your child's doormat, or you are demonstrating servanthood parenting. Put a **D** by the **Doormat** statements and a **SP** by the statements that reflect **Servanthood** parenting.

1. _____ Dad, this shirt's dirty and I want to wear it today. Okay, son, let me wash it right away.

2. _____ Mom, would you please get off the computer. I want to play "Air Guitar" with my friends. Sure, sweetheart. I can finish this financial spreadsheet later.

3. _____ Tommy, I'm taking this food box over to the homeless shelter. Want to come with me?

4. _____ No, mama. I'm not giving up any of my old toys. I might play with them later. Okay, darling.

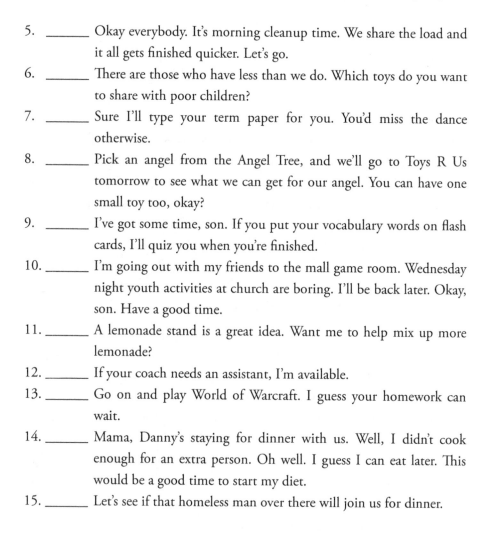

5. _____ Okay everybody. It's morning cleanup time. We share the load and it all gets finished quicker. Let's go.

6. _____ There are those who have less than we do. Which toys do you want to share with poor children?

7. _____ Sure I'll type your term paper for you. You'd miss the dance otherwise.

8. _____ Pick an angel from the Angel Tree, and we'll go to Toys R Us tomorrow to see what we can get for our angel. You can have one small toy too, okay?

9. _____ I've got some time, son. If you put your vocabulary words on flash cards, I'll quiz you when you're finished.

10. _____ I'm going out with my friends to the mall game room. Wednesday night youth activities at church are boring. I'll be back later. Okay, son. Have a good time.

11. _____ A lemonade stand is a great idea. Want me to help mix up more lemonade?

12. _____ If your coach needs an assistant, I'm available.

13. _____ Go on and play World of Warcraft. I guess your homework can wait.

14. _____ Mama, Danny's staying for dinner with us. Well, I didn't cook enough for an extra person. Oh well. I guess I can eat later. This would be a good time to start my diet.

15. _____ Let's see if that homeless man over there will join us for dinner.

Jesus spent three years equipping his disciples to carry on in his absence. As parents, we typically have eighteen to twenty-one years to "train our children up in the ways of the Lord." Certain tools for effective parenting will help us continually affirm who's in charge in the family and achieve our goal of "training up" our children. These tools include the following:

Taking our leadership jointly and personally.
Acknowledging and abiding by the developmental stages of parenting

Being consistent and timely.

Defining roles and expectations.

Setting guidelines with target behaviors, rewards, consequences

Parental Leadership

Parents are given this blessing of birth jointly. Our leadership in the family is also a joint appointment. And yet, each of us has unique qualities, experiences, and character to bring to the table. As parents, we must negotiate who's in charge continually, based on availability, circumstances, and the unique challenges of the moment. Paul told the church at Ephesus, "Husbands and wives, submit to one another (Eph. 5:21)." This passage precedes the more famous passages of, "Wives, submit to your husbands (Eph. 5:22), and, "Husbands, treat your wives just as Christ treats the church (Eph. 5:25)." Our togetherness as parents precedes our individual leadership in the family.

An enduring myth of parenting is that we must present a united front to our children. This is a myth simply because it is unattainable. We are changing creatures, affected by internal and external circumstances on an on-going basis. We come from different parenting models. Parenting is the most important job for which we never have any formal training. However, rather than a curse, our unique contribution to the joint leadership of parenting is a blessing. Our differences teach our children to adapt to varying leadership styles. Our differences also promote opportunities to learn from each other. If I am a softy on bedtime and you are not, I want to learn how you do it, so I have an easier time when it's my turn to put the children to bed.

Finally, any pressure to conform to unity in parenting is a setup to fail. Remembering all the rules and agreements, amidst the continual flux of circumstance, becomes arduous at best, more likely simply impossible. Jesus became God made flesh for this very reason. The Scribes and Pharisees of the Jewish church had morphed the Ten Commandments into over 1300 rules and regulations for good Jews to follow. Jesus clarified his ministry by indicating that he had not come to replace the law, but to fulfill it (Matt. 5:17). Later, he broke it down by indicating that all law is fulfilled by loving God with all your heart, mind, and soul, and by loving others as you love yourself (Rom. 13:9-

10). As parents, we succeed not so much with hard and fast rules, as with love. Our love for our children and ourselves takes into consideration the individual strengths and weaknesses of each parent, as well as the time and circumstances of the children.

As our children grew up, my wife and I developed what we called "tag team parenting." The available parent takes care of the immediate situation with full authority. However, when possible, your spouse is around if you need back-up. When the available parent is loaded down with their own "stuff" and stressed out, or when the parenting exchange is going nowhere, that parent is free to find your spouse, explain the situation, and say, "Tag, you're it."

Tag team parenting embodies the concept of taking parental leadership both personally and jointly. Each of you has a personal history, experience with your own parents, and personal observations of others from which you derive your parenting style. You are your own expert on parenting your children. You know when you are "on" and when you've "had it." Monitoring your effectiveness helps you bring your personal best to the parenting experience.

On the other hand, thank God that He intended us to parent jointly. Single parents are my heroes, because parenting is exhausting even under the best of circumstances. Joint leadership in parenting allows us to give each other a break, so that our children always get the best of us. It also allows us to confer with each other on the big issues. Even the most compliant and obedient children are going to try to manipulate and evoke power struggles when given the opportunity. When a child goes to one parent for permission and is told "no," they will go to the other parent for a second opinion. If the parents are not conferring, the child may get permission at the risk of rife and discontent between the parents.

Children seem to be born with the automatic retort, "Mommy said I could," when told "No" by daddy, and vice versa. These types of exchanges will evoke manipulation and power struggle if the parents don't confer. Not every request from a child requires an immediate response. "Let me talk with your mother and one of us will get back with you," is a healthy parenting response that defuses the likelihood of manipulation and power struggle. As children observe parents to be in synchrony, exercising joint parenting leadership, each parent's personal parenting leadership is enhanced as well.

Developmental Stages of Parenting

Children need different styles of parenting at different ages. The emphasis of parenting changes with the developmental stages of children. Erik Erickson's work defining the psychosocial developmental stages of children (Erickson, 1950), and Lawrence Kohlberg's work defining the development of cognitive functioning and reasoning capacity (Kohlberg, 1958) are excellent resources for parents to keep pace with their children's needs, according to their ages.

Hands-On Parenting

From birth to about age 5, children are almost totally dependent on parents for everything. Babies can't change their own diapers. Toddlers can't tie their own shoes, although the advent of Velcro almost negates this as a developmental milestone. Preschoolers have trouble telling time. These and other tasks require full hands-on parenting for children who are newborn to age 5. Each event is a teachable moment with your child.

While this stage of parenting requires lots of pure direction, parents need to break down directions and tasks to basic, step-by-step, concrete instruction. Parental emphasis is on keeping the child physically safe, while also helping them explore their environment and expand their knowledge base. Researchers conclude that about 80% of a child's personality and temperament is formed by the time they are age 5. As parents, we are the primary source for these developments. Hands-on parenting from birth to age 5 affords our children the optimal experience to grow physically, emotionally, and spiritually in safety.

Directed Parenting

When children enter school, all bets are off. Their knowledge base and breadth of experience is exponentially expanded. As parents, our influence becomes one of many sources. We will hear our 8-year old child protest, "but Mooooom, Anna's mom got her a cell phone. Alll the kids have one…I'll be the ooonly kid in my class without one. Puhleeeeese?"

From ages 6 to 12, Erickson talks about children developing industry (Erickson, 1950) their world has expanded greatly and they are realizing that they are a force in that world. With the rapid fire requests/demands parents will get from their children between these ages, the value of joint parental leadership and tag team parenting is optimal. Conferring with one another keeps you from being the good guy/bad guy parents. Conferring strengthens your resolve to avoid power struggles and manipulation. Practice the response, "What part of 'No' did you not understand?"

Because children this age are developing industry, further exploring their environments, becoming more interactive, and forming opinions and perspectives, it is also important to begin negotiating with your children. All requests are teachable moments. Instead of an automatic yes or no, include your child in the discussion of the pros and cons of granting their request. Help them formulate the steps, practicalities, cost/benefit ratio of their request. This is known as the Socratic teaching method, named after the Greek philosopher who was known for never giving a straight answer. He asked lots of questions of his students in an enduring effort to help them think for themselves, the ultimate goal of parenting as well.

When challenged, and you will be challenged by your child at this stage, give a rationale. Explain your conclusions, Listen to your child's perspective. One of the worst parental responses to a child's request/protest is, "Because I said so." The rationale is the heart of directed parenting. You do have the ultimate authority. You do direct your child. Tell them where to be, what to do, when to be home, when to go to bed. However, providing rationale for your direction gives your child context, comfort, and expanded understanding. Providing rationale for your direction adds earned authority to your ascribed authority.

Children this age are most receptive to family meetings, also known as family councils. They like being included in the decision-making process, having their opinions heard. Parents can call council meetings to problem-solve chore completion, allowance issues, family rules and expectations. Such meetings give you opportunity to role model joint parenting leadership, while also reinforcing the value of the children's opinions and perspective.

Parents will want to confer before calling the meeting; to be sure you are on the same page. Someone will need to be the recorder, writing down family agreements and attending rewards and consequences. Each person will need to get a copy of the concluding document, and agreements will need to be posted on the family message board. The document becomes interactive, fluid, with revisions made as necessary and follow-up meetings called as needed for review. This kind of inclusion reinforces your earned parenting authority. Outcomes such as contracts and job descriptions are less helpful products of ascribed authority.

Parental Advisement

From ages 12 to 18, parents increasingly offer advice to children. While you continue to have the ultimate authority, offering advice encourages your teenager to develop responsibility and independence, the core developmental tasks of this age range. With your child's increasing age and emotional maturity, parenting becomes less directed and more collaborative.

Kohlberg notes that children begin to understand abstractions by age 12 (Kohlberg, 1958). Directed parenting addresses your child's capacity to think concretely. Parental advice addresses your child's capacity to think abstractly. Your advice comes from your experience, years, and wisdom. You make effort to understand teenage lingo (texting short-hand still baffles me, LOL), fashion, and friendship circles.

Your boundaries and expectations are crystal clear, but you give your teenager lots of leash. As the tether lengthens, you advise your teen of possibilities, options, and ways to responsibly reach their goals. Because teens are expanding their friendship networks, you advise them of interactive factors, ulterior motives, clique dynamics, as well as the social network exchanges of strangers, acquaintances, friends, best friends, and the cost/benefit of each kind of exchange. In healthy families, one or both parents become the teen's secret mountaintop guru, a fount of wisdom and advice whom no one knows about, because it's "uncool" to be able to talk to your dad/mom "like that."

Where conflict arises, with consideration of threat/safety and intensity of outcome, teens are "allowed" to fail. Parents position themselves to "catch" their teen when they fail, to help them understand the process, and to learn from their experience. Research is clear that we learn much more from periodic failure than we do from repeated success. Avoid the tendency to prematurely rescue your teen from anticipated failure. Such action undermines the teen's sense of self-worth and self-confidence. Avoid the dreaded "I told you so," at all costs. You are providing a learning experience for your teen, not a display of your power, wisdom, or control. With failure, offer your teen a debriefing experience with such questions as, "Wanna talk about it?" "What do you think you could have done differently to gain a better outcome?"

When offering advice, do so only after you have listened to and elicited all of your teen's feelings and perspective. Then suggest, "I have some thoughts about your situation. Can I share them with you?" This symbolic act of asking permission reinforces your earned authority, while also respecting your teen's growing individuality. Rather than directly advise, "I think you should do X," consider ways to make your perspective more palatable. "I once knew another teenager in a similar situation. Wanna hear what he did?" When your advice gets rejected for whatever reason, return to empathy. It is okay if your teen is not ready or in a place to hear your counsel. Sometimes the best we can do for our kids is to offer their angst up to God in prayer.

Consultative Parenting

As our children become adults, from age 18 and on, we try to move from mentor to consultant. In doing so, we have no stake in the outcome. Full authority and responsibility rest with our adult child. We have transitioned to helpful friend who knows when to prod and when to back off.

Research on effective industry consultation defines three key points. The effective consultant first has or acquires all the available expertise in their field of consultation. Then, they acquire all the specific data to address the particular consultation request thoroughly. Finally, they set a time and place to present their findings and recommendations to the decision-maker(s) in the company. There is no personal stake in whether the company accepts the consultant's recommendations or not.

Similarly, as a consultative parent, you wait for your adult child to come to you. You ask or find all the relevant data and context. You get permission to present your findings and recommendations. You leave. For even well-intentioned parents, it's the leaving part that is hardest. Because you have successfully raised an independent and responsible adult by this time, your leaving the outcome to him conveys the love and respect that are the hallmarks of healthy relationships.

These developmental stages of parenting complement Erickson's psychosocial stages and Kohlberg's stages of cognitive development and reasoning. Children are not expected to do or be any more than fits their stage of development. Parents continue a process of pacing/leading, and making the most of teachable moments, while reaching their goal of re-birthing responsible, independent adults, who then transition to mature friends.

Learning the Concept: Exercise 7, Developmental Stages of Parenting

Adapting your parenting style to the age of your child both ensures nurturance and safety, and enhances the parent-child relationship. Developmental stages of parenting coincide with the developing skill and relational abilities of your children. Children from birth to age 5 require hands-on parenting, as everything is new to them. Elementary school age children need to be directed in their activities. Middle School and High School youth rail against being told what to do and will respond better to advice, where they understand you have the final word, but their perspective and opinions are important to you. College-age and your children who are now adults benefit from your wise counsel in a consultative parenting model.

Look at the following quotes. Determine the approximate age of the child based on the parenting style shown in the quote. In the space to the left for each item, put **HO** for preschool **Hands On**, **D** for elementary school age **Directed Parenting**, **A** for middle school/high school age **Advice-Based Parenting**, and **C** for college and adult children **Consultative Parenting**.

1. _____ Which girl do you like the best, son?
2. _____ I think working along on that term paper will be less pressure on you and help you get a higher grade than pulling an all-nighter before it's due.
3. _____ Here, let me carry that glass to the table for you.

4. _____ You know, sweetheart, we are a reflection of the company we keep. I don't want you to play with Susie for a while. Let's build some other friendships.

5. _____ Take my hand and let's look both ways before we cross this road, okay?

6. _____ When I was offered two jobs, I wrote down the pros and cons of each so I could size up what would be best for me.

7. _____ You think coach will let you play if you skip practice? I want you to go to practice.

8. _____ You can go to the school dance by yourself if you want to. I remember having more fun at my school dances when I brought a date.

9. _____ You want me to build you a downhill racer? Let me show you how to do it and we'll work on it together.

10. _____ You're doing your pee dance again. Let's go to the potty.

11. _____ Stop. Look both ways. A bicycle and a truck collide. Who walks away from that?

12. _____ I think your tomboy friend has blossomed into a girl. Let me tell you about girls.

13. _____ When I was in college, I majored in what I was good at, and the rest is history.

14. _____ Don't you need braces underneath the floor? I don't want your tree house falling.

Being Consistent and Timely

Healthy parents are consistent and timely in parenting their children. These concepts speak to the adaptability and fluidity of parenting. With acknowledgement to the myth of providing a unified front, parents nonetheless try to be internally consistent, even if they parent the children differently. To the extent that parents are collaborative, consistency will increase. Because children offer problems/issues in rapid fire succession, timeliness helps parents track problems and address the most urgent first. To the extent that parents are observant, ask questions, and on top of things, timeliness will increase.

Parents learn over time to adapt to each child's temperament and circumstances. If a younger sibling is more emotionally mature at a certain age than her older sister was at that same age, the younger child might be better able to handle a certain privilege earlier than the older child did. Consistency between siblings is less important than adapting responses to specific children and circumstances.

Setting up rules and expectations ahead of time increases the likelihood of consistency in parenting, while also limiting parent-child conflict. In the Bowers family, Jim and Lauren had allowed Emily to go to youth group gatherings at the church at age 15. One night, they found out that she attended an after-party at a girlfriend's home without permission. Even though she called to let them know where she was, her parents gave her consequences on her return home. Emily protested, "If I had known I was going to be punished, I would have come straight home."

When younger brother Jason came along and encountered the same circumstances, his folks more clearly outlined their rules and expectations, along with attending rewards and consequences ahead of time, thereby alleviating subsequent conflict and distance. While it would be impossible to anticipate all potential pitfalls, parents are wise to front-end their rules and expectations as much as possible.

Research in behavioral change shows that the more timely the response, the more rapid the learning. Children who grow up with, "When your father gets home, he's going to wail the tar out of you," are more likely to repeat their errors even though they may be more severely punished. Delaying the consequence causes a disconnect with the crime, animosity with the punishing parent, and lower self-esteem for the offending child.

I encourage parents to keep a visual image in mind. My left hand is stationary and represents the point in time where your child broke the rule. My right hand is movable and represents your parental response to the broken rule. The greater the distance between my hands, the greater the conflict and trouble you buy in "training up" your child. Since I can move my right hand, I choose to place it as close to my left hand as possible. That is, I want to respond as quickly to the rule infraction as possible, thereby helping my child connect the punishment to the crime, while maintaining a positive relationship with me and keeping his strong self-esteem.

Finally, timeliness refers to addressing the most recent problem first. Frequently, children compound the problem. If Gracie smacks Jason and then lies about it by denying it, there are two problems. The lie takes precedence over the violence because it is more recent. Both problems are addressed with consequences. The lesson here is to ask the offending child how much trouble she wants. If she had a choice between having two problems or one problem, which would she choose? Timeliness in parenting minimizes the number of problems to address.

Defining Roles and Expectations

Jim returned with Jason from a quick trip to the library. He settled his son down to study, and then went to Grace's bedroom. Emily was there, reading her little sister a bedtime story.

"Hey, Punkin," Jim hailed as he came into the room.

Grace threw her covers off and bounded out of the bed to greet her daddy. "Daddy!" she squealed in delight. "Look at all my Band-Aids. I was bleeding all down my leg."

"Wow. That must have hurt lots," Jim replied.

"Naah. Emily helped me clean it up and stick the Band-Aids." Her big sister rolled her eyes as Grace dramatized the events.

"Well, sweetheart," Jim scooped his younger daughter into his arms, "Now you know how dangerous it is to play with sharp things."

"I didn't know the razor was sharp. I just saw mommy and sis getting the shaving cream off their legs with it and I wanted to be big too."

"You'll be big soon enough, Gracie. Don't rush it." Jim began to tickle her. "When you are big, it will make me a geezer."

Grace squealed in delight and countered, "You already are, Daddy."

Emily got up from the edge of her sister's bed and began to leave the room. "If you're on duty here, Dad, I've got some more homework to finish."

"Thanks for pitching in, honey," Jim called over his shoulder to Emily as they passed each other. He carried Grace to her bed and then tucked her in.

"I'm glad you are safe now, Gracie, and that all you got was a little bloody." Grace squirmed in her bed as her daddy spoke. "But," Jim continued, "You could have really been hurt. You know better than to play with sharp things like razors."

"I know," Grace admitted, dropping her chin to her chest and looking penitent.

"Okay, time to go to sleep," Jim concluded. "You mother and I will talk about this tonight, and there may be consequences for you tomorrow."

"What? Not fair," Grace protested.

"Gracie, you know the rules about playing safe and asking permission when in doubt," her daddy admonished. "Did you play safe when you tried to shave your legs? Did you ask permission to use the razor?"

"No, sir." Grace admitted, with dramatic flair.

"Okay, then. We'll talk tomorrow, and you think about what might be a fair consequence." Jim kissed his daughter on the forehead.

"Okaaay," Grace agreed reluctantly. "G'nite, daddy." She snuggled into her covers as her father left and closed the door behind him.

This vignette captures the essence of family rules and expectations. The easier path for Jim to take would have been to check on Grace after getting back from the library, be relieved that she is okay, and then simply drop the matter. Many parents would lose a teachable moment in doing so. Not only that, but avoiding or ignoring Grace's rule violation would have emboldened her to break this or other rules in the future. As parents develop rules and expectations for the family, they help build responsible, independent adults, the overarching goal of effective parenting.

Learning the Concept: Exercise 8, Defining Roles and Expectations

Take a moment, individually, as a couple, or in a family meeting, and write out a job description for each family member. Include in each job description an approximation of time used per activity for the 24-hour day. Be sure to conclude each job description with a time allotted, open-ended statement about "will complete other activities as needed and directed." Pass the job descriptions among family members for comment and discussion. Have you missed any regular activities that take time out of the day? Have you accounted for sleep time? For travel time? For personal time? For time with God?

Now write down all the jobs, chores, and activities it takes just for your home to run smoothly and look nice. Brainstorm and look for any items, however big or small. Did you ever imagine all that goes into running your home?

Now match the roles (job descriptions) with the expectations (jobs, chores, expectations) to draft a plan of who does what, when, where, and how. The matching will not be perfect. Some expectations will be joint or family attention, rather than assigned to one person. Other expectations will be limited in assignment by age and capability of the people in the family.

Family Meetings

Parents need to talk to each other about what they want their children to do and how they want them to act. This can happen most effectively in the context of two types of family meetings. Even toddlers can benefit from family meetings, as long as rules and expectations are conveyed in terms they can understand.

Regularly scheduled, maintenance-focused, family meetings are one type. Jan Miksovsky (USA Weekend, 2011), co-founder of Cozi.com, put together the online family calendar and organizer. These meetings become a family gathering that each of you can count on. Sunday afternoons, for about an hour, is often the week's most down time for activities. These meetings work best with some kind of agenda. Miksovsky recommends starting these meetings with Thank-Yous. Each family member thanks another or something in the past week. Another nice touch would be to include a roundtable discussion of gratitude.

Meetings then continue with White-Board Items. You keep a white-board throughout the week on which any family member can jot down problems as they come up. This gives you immediate release from the frustration and assurance that your problem will be discussed at the next family meeting. During the white-board part of the meeting, solutions to these problems are discussed. Every family member has a voice.

Also, regularly scheduled family meetings include the agenda item of reviewing the upcoming family calendar. When everybody has a heads-up on events or activities that impact them, the family runs more smoothly.

Finally, weekly family meetings offer an opportunity to recognize contributions of all family members, providing rewards and privileges accordingly.

The other important kind of family meeting is targeted and designed to tackle a particular problem that is affecting the family. After a preliminary discussion between you to agree on the scope and intent of this family meeting, give the children enough time to accommodate you and then call the meeting. Such meetings are excellent tools for discussion of rules and expectations, chore lists, as well as planning for individual and family events.

Family meetings reinforce parental authority. To be effective, they need to be interactive, with particular emphasis on coaxing ideas from each of the children. If children conclude that family meetings simply provide a forum for parents coming down on them or telling them what to do, then the intent and impact will be lost and greater emotional distance between parents and children will result.

Family meetings are specific, concrete, and time limited. As children understand the rationale and see it as benefiting them, they will buy into the concept. Parents want to facilitate discussion and promote/probe for feelings. The intent and enthusiasm quickly erode if meetings are allowed to drift into complaining, criticizing, attacking, and defending.

In starting targeted family meetings, get input from everybody as to the topic and hoped for outcome. As each person's goal for the meeting is addressed and reached, the meeting value will rise. With topical agreement, you next want to facilitate a brainstorming of options/activities related to the topic.

For example, when a family meeting is called to define and assign chores, the topical question would be, "what chore activities need our attention on a daily or weekly basis so that we can live together comfortably and be fair about who does what?" Then, parents encourage a brainstorming of these possible activities, adding to the list and also encouraging each child's contribution as well. The concept of brainstorming includes offering free-floating ideas without critiquing or editorializing, until the ideas are exhausted.

Following brainstorming, review the list of ideas/chores with an eye toward who does what, and why the choices make sense. This part represents the "nuts and bolts" of the family meeting. Therefore, most importantly, the outcomes need to be specific, concrete, and well defined.

As choices and agreements are made, define both the time frame and way in which the meeting outcome will be implemented and when its effectiveness will be reviewed. The first review needs to be relatively short, say in a week, to maintain the momentum of a positive family meeting. Conclude the meeting with a comment such as, "Okay, let's experiment and try these things for a week before deciding whether they will work for the family. We can modify them, if need be then, to best fit all of us."

Finally, in implementing the agreements of family meetings, write out the agreements, lists, or other outcomes, post one copy and give a copy to each family member. Children are notorious for complaining, "You didn't say that," "That's not what we agreed on," "I don't remember that." If the outcomes and agreements are written down, there is less room for interpretation and error.

Family meetings promote an atmosphere of family connection, cooperating for the individual and common good. Such meetings help reinforce parental authority, clarify each person's role in the family, and define expectations. They also reduce the likelihood of manipulation and power struggles within the family. Finally, they reinforce the family as a unit, where all family members play important roles for the family to function efficiently and for each member to grow in the ways of the Lord.

Setting Guidelines, with Target Behaviors, Rewards, and Consequences

A specific variation of family meetings involves developing a behavior management system, specifically designed to help children focus their efforts in personal growth and development. However, most such systems are individualized, and therefore the product of discussion between the parents and a particular child (See Appendix 4). A modified family meeting could be called, but only if the parents want all of their children to work on the same target behavior(s). Because of age and stage differences among most siblings in a family, this modified family meeting is unlikely. Behavior management systems are typically child-specific.

When you notice a repetitive behavior or attitude that is not working for your child, alert your spouse and both of you commit your concern to prayer. Agree with one another to notice and monitor the concern for a few weeks. A rule of thumb is that most negative behavior will self-correct in a couple of weeks. If the behavior is noticeable for four to six weeks, then it may be a problem for your child, rather than just a mood.

After monitoring for a while, if you agree to put together a behavior management system to help your child address your concern, then jointly go to him with your concern. For the Bowers, Lauren had noticed for a while that Jason had been holing up in his room after school and through until bedtime for several weeks. She had to ask him to come to dinner each night. He seemed distant and angry a lot. She and Jim talked about her concerns on several occasions and Jim concurred with her after noticing these behaviors as well.

Lauren brought her concerns to Jason's attention on several occasions, but he would blow her off, and otherwise minimize the behavior. Jason also had begun taunting Grace and putting down Emily. Lauren talked with him about her concerns, asking if everything were all right. Jason always protested that everything was fine and all she wanted to do was be in his business. Several punishments for bad attitude or disrespect seemed to do no good. Lauren observed that Jason had stopped going to youth group activities at church. He also had picked up a new best friend outside of church. Lauren and Jim decided to implement a behavior management system with their son.

Define the Target Behavior

Children will "buy into" a behavior management system to the extent that they fully understand the target behavior and have input into the development of rewards and consequences. Many parents err by identifying a vague, broad, undefined target behavior and linking it to only one, usually magnanimous reward or hideous consequence. Frequently, I've heard parents lament that their child was a bright student, but failing in school. The dad would say, "I told him that, if his grades came up we'd all go to Disney World. If he didn't pull them up, I would ground him until he is thirty." The children on whom such a vague behavior management system is imposed will be doomed to failure. Effective parenting occurs when your child buys into the vehicle of positive growth and change (Furman & Beuer, 2009).

Most children will salivate over such a great reward, but be unable to attain it both because the target behavior is not specific and the reward is too distant. After a while, the disgruntled child gives up on the task and rationalizes, "I didn't want to go to Disney World anyway." Also, most parents won't follow through on the extreme consequence. Both parent and child end up frustrated and defeated.

In contrast, when the target behavior is clearly and concretely defined, and rewards are imminently attainable, even the most dug in, recalcitrant child will buy into the system. As the parent, your initial goal is to help your child guarantee success. Accordingly, re-tool the target behavior from "your grades have to come up" to "I want you to show me passing grades in math over the next two weeks, and I will help you with homework and study for quizzes and tests, so that you can reach your goal."

Collaborate on Rewards and Consequences

Once the target behavior is re-tooled to be specific, clear, and concrete, and then build incentive for your child to want to change his behavior. For the Bowers, Lauren and Jim told Jason that they wanted him to return to youth group, invite his new friend to join him in the youth group, spend "hang time" with other friends in addition to his new friend, compliment his sister Emily, and spend a total of one hour per week playing with his younger sister Grace. Jason was not thrilled at these new "burdens." He told his folks that they just wanted to ruin his life, control whom he sees, and not have any fun.

Even with this level of target behavior specificity, children will not do what's important to you if it is not also important to them. Collaborating on the rewards and consequences ups the ante for your child. Most children will trash even the most elegant reward if it is unattainable.

Collaborating with your child to develop a list of ten reward options will make it ten times as hard to negate. Anything that the child wants can be on the list, subject to your time and financial constraints. Most children light up with excitement and anticipation when you agree with their options. With their rewards in sight, children will buy into attaining the target behavior because now doing so has become important to them.

Similarly, develop together a list of ten consequences, of varying intensity. The consequences also need to be age and stage specific. That is, Jim and Lauren might put Grace, at age 8, in the corner for twenty minutes, but not Jason, who is age 15. They might limit Jason's video game time, whereas Emily could care less about playing video games. When children add to the consequence list, they tend to be harder on themselves than their parents do. Adding to the list also increases the child's accountability and responsibility in reaching the target behavior. There are no levels of consequences, nor "easy" ones, but having ten provides variety and keeps your child's attention.

Tracking Success

Many parents will use a variation of a chart or checklist to track success. For children ages 12 or younger, the Good Kid Chart (See Appendix 4) is a kid-friendly vehicle to track success. Target behaviors are listed in the left-hand column. List them in positive terms, because people naturally work toward positive goals. Thus, "Don't hit" becomes "Play nice."

To sustain momentum and attention, the chart is reviewed daily. When a target behavior is achieved for that day, the chart is marked accordingly. The first level of consequence for children is simply not marking the chart for that target behavior. When the target behavior is obliterated, then the child is directed to his consequence list to pick his consequence. The violation has to be egregious to warrant a consequence.

For example, If Jason is to play with Grace each day for no less than 15 minutes, and he knocks her down and breaks her toys, then he failed that target behavior so severely that he gets no mark and picks a consequence.

For Jason, his folks have identified five target behaviors. He might only have to attain marks on three of the five at first, to help assure success, in order for Jason to pick a reward for the day. As he achieves more success, his criteria for reward might increase from 3 of 5, ultimately to 5 of 5. When he routinely succeeds with a certain target behavior, congratulate his success and remove the target behavior from the chart. That gives him opportunity to focus more on the harder goals. It also gives his parents opportunity to add another target behavior they would like Jason to work on. Thus the chart has a certain fluidity that keeps it current and meaningful.

To help your child integrate the target behaviors into their temperament and ongoing interactions, develop two reward lists. One list is available to your child on a daily basis. As he strings several good days together through a week, he would be able to choose a bigger reward from the weekly reward list.

For example, a younger child might be able to stay up a half hour later as a daily reward. As he strings several good days together, he might be able to have a sleepover or go to a movie on the weekend as a weekly reward. The linking of both short-term and longer-term rewards helps your child buy into the behavior management system and incorporate the target behaviors into their on-going temperament and behavioral interactions.

Learning the Concept

Appendix 4 provides a description, rationale, and procedural guide to utilizing "The Good Kid Chart." This chart, and attending posters, provides an effective system for identifying target behavior, rewards, and consequences. It maximizes the cooperation of your child, helps him change unhealthy behavior, and reach his goals more efficiently and quickly. It is a mechanism that focuses on collaboration, where your child will own the change process.

Review this Appendix with your spouse and children. Talk about how such a behavior chart might be implemented in your home.

SUMMARY

God calls us to be good stewards of our time, talent, and energies. He calls parents to be his emissaries to our children. The popular wristband, "What Would Jesus Do?" was more than a fad cliché. We need to draw on our individual and joint resources to parent effectively. We strive to merge ascribed and earned authority in parenting. We modify our parenting style to accommodate our children's ages and stages. We use teachable moments and parental direction to reach our ultimate goal of launching, Christ-centered, independent, and responsible adults into a foreboding world.

On our journey, certain parenting tools will clearly define who's in charge, while also smoothing out the bumps in the road. First, take seriously the formidable task of providing parental leadership to your family. Parenting is the hardest job for which you will never have formal training. Draw on your own and each other's well of emotional and experiential resource to be the best parents you can be.

Second, keep pace with your child's age/stage-related needs and expectations, and modify your parental approach accordingly. Third, be consistent and timely with what you say and do with your children. Children can get so lost and confused by words and actions. Break it down for them. Make it simple. Fourth, clearly define the roles and expectations for each family member. Regular family meetings are a helpful tool to help everybody keep current.

Finally, where consistent difficulty arises, use a clear behavior management strategy that defines target behaviors in positive terms, provides timely reward and consequence accordingly, and tracks success as our children consistently reach these target behaviors.

Lord, help me to get out of your way. Have my children see you in my words and actions with them. I am humbled by the daunting task of being Christ-like in my children's eyes. Give me your grace and strength to live out the authority and leadership You have called me to lead my family. I accept your gifts and ask you to help me pass them on to my children, to your glory. Amen.

Chapter Three

Children will Always
Test the Limits

I n the thirty-five years of my clinical practice, thousands of children and teens have come through my office. They have varying issues, including anxiety, depression, impulse control disorders, as well as problems with emerging identity, school and authority problems. They all come to me with one or both parents, or caregivers, by their side. Within five minutes of the first session, I have a good idea of how the parent interacts with their child and how the child tests the limits.

All children and teens will test the limits of most situations, especially where parents are involved. Does this mean we have a generation of bad seeds running rampant? No. Testing the limits is natural for young people. It is in testing limits that they define the boundaries of expectation and assure their security and safety. Testing limits is not only natural, but also essential to the maturation process.

However, the goal for our children is not freedom. Rather, the goal is the security and certainty that the limits are there.

Nothing is more anxiety-inducing than unrestricted freedom for a child. They do not have the emotional nor cognitive maturity to accept freedom and make good choices. At least until age 12, when Kohlberg's age of abstract reasoning kicks in, and parents move from directed parenting to advisement, children will grow and thrive best with reasonable limits on their behaviors. Consider the following vignette.

Morning Routine at the Bowers' Home

"Jaaasonnn. Are you up yet?" Jim bellowed from the kitchen. "Breakfast is almost ready."

Jason stirred in his bed. He lifted his head to check the time on his bedside clock radio. The heavy metal music had erupted beside him fifteen minutes ago, but only now was permeating the dense fog of sleep. His head fell with a thud back onto his pillow. He rationalized that he could sleep ten more minutes, and then hurry to the bus stop.

"Jason?" Jim had moved from the kitchen to the bottom of the stairs. "Come on, son. Let's don't start the morning this way again," he pleaded. "Your oat meal is getting cold."

Ugh. I hate oatmeal. Jason thought, *what's with dad and oatmeal?* His mind drifted to an open field, horses galloping in the distance. He was leaning over the fence trying to get their attention, when he noticed a heavy, oatmeal feed bag draped around his neck.

"Jason," Jim called sternly again from the bottom of the stairs.

Wait…wait…I've got a few more seconds of snooze, he calculated.

"If I have to come up there, young man," Jim started to ascend the stairs.

Okay, now. Jason swept the covers off him and popped out of bed. "I'm up, Dad, I'm up." Jim leaned in his bedroom door. "Geesh, Dad, don't get your shorts all bunched up," Jason complained, as he shed his pajamas and began getting dressed. Jim sighed and turned to resume kitchen duty.

Meanwhile, in the kitchen, Lauren was tending to Grace. She was always a ray of sunshine in the morning, full of questions. She had gotten up early so she could enjoy the girl time with her mom. Emily, on the other hand, had a senior honors class at school before her first period, so she had dressed, fed herself, and was out the door a half hour ago. Usually, Emily was first shift for breakfast, then Grace, and Jason breezed through for the third breakfast shift. Lauren just tried to keep up.

"Mommy," Grace mused as she pushed her boiled egg around in its bowl, "Why is it light when I have to go to bed and dark when I have to get up? Isn't that backwards?"

"Why, yes, sweetheart, it is backwards," Lauren concluded. She sat down across from Grace at the kitchen table, getting ready to dig in to her fruit bowl.

"Then change it back, mommy." Grace directed.

"Well, honey, it's not that easy. Sometimes the simplest things are hardest to do."

Grace pushed her bowl away from her. "Yuck. I don't like this egg. It's squishy inside. Can I have cereal instead?"

Lauren sighed as she rose to get the cereal from the pantry. She resumed her explanation as she fixed Grace a bowl of cereal. "You see, Grace, it's now daylight savings time. That means the sun goes down later…"

Grace heard Jason's bus honking its horn outside. She ran to the window to watch his mad dash out the front door. "Whoa. Right over that bush. Good jump, bro. And here comes dad with Jason's book bag. There's the hand-off," she continued her play-by-play, "Oooh, Jason's in trouble now."

Lauren put the cereal on the table at Grace's place. "Come on, Gracie," she urged, "Your time is running short now too. Come eat."

Grace returned from the window. She looked at her cereal, and then at her mom's fruit bowl. "Nah, I think I want your fruit bowl." She switched her bowl with her mom's and began devouring the fruit. Lauren rolled her eyes, sighed, and thought, *and to think that I went to all that schooling just to do shift work and become a short order cook.*

Boundaries and Choices

In their own ways, both Jason and Grace are making bad choices. However, the permeable boundaries set by their parents actually promote these bad choices.

When boundaries are clear and consistent, children respond with better choices and less drama. Both Jason and Grace are plucking their parents' nerves and enjoying their power. These may not be conscious, intentional goals by the kids, but they set the stage for conflict. Yet, it doesn't have to be this way.

In this family scenario, the stage is set for a family meeting around morning routine to re-tool boundaries and expectations. When needs and feelings are clearly expressed and understood, parents can define re-tooled boundaries that will be accepted by the children. Natural consequences, then, define whether children are making good or bad choices in response to these boundaries.

For example, when Jason complains that he likes to sleep as long as possible before getting up each school morning and the parents define their need to provide a nutritious meal for the kids each morning, then a meeting of the minds is possible. Jason could go to bed earlier to get his allotted sleep. He could set three alarm clocks set in intervals and strategically placed toward his bathroom to conquer the "rack monster" each morning. With the boundary set that he must be seated in the kitchen by a certain time to get breakfast at home, Jim is relieved of his worry and cajoling, and Jason gets a less hectic start to his school days. As a backup plan, the Bowers could sign Jason up for a school breakfast, but Jason would have to pay for it out of his allowance or other personal resources when he is too late to have breakfast at home and make the school bus. Additionally, if he misses breakfast and/or the bus, then "hard labor" of some sort is the consequence.

Similarly, Grace gets by a lot on the "cute factor." Lauren doesn't even realize how much she is being played by her bundle of joy. She would be less weary and have a less stressed start to her work day by defining boundaries and expectations for Grace. Perhaps she and Grace could talk together about breakfast options the night before. When Grace makes her choice, among equally nutritious and healthy options, then the rule is "finish what you chose and no take-backs." When Grace cops an attitude, consequences follow for her bad choices.

Granted that these are simplistic solutions and circumstances may be more complicated, but the general rule remains. With clear, concise boundaries and expectations, along with defined natural consequences, children are more likely to make good choices. Additionally, they are more secure, less anxious, and relieved to not be in charge when the limits are there.

Permeable or inconsistent boundaries make for bad choices by children. Healthy boundaries are well-defined, consistent, and enforced by both parents. They are firm limits to which children will respond and for which they will be relieved. Boundaries are set by parents in Christ-centered families. Just as Jesus showed us how to live, we too in turn show our children through loving, set boundaries.

Choices, healthy or not, are made by children. When left to their own devices, such choices are oftentimes bad. When guided by parents and directed by firm boundaries, such choices are oftentimes good. Children make good choices when they know what the limits are to their behavior. Children are relieved when the tested limit is secure and they are not forced to be in charge of their lives.

Learning the Concept: Exercise 9, Boundaries and Choices

Look at the following comments. Determine whether the comment applies to a **Boundary (B)** or to a **Choice (C)**. Mark accordingly on the space to the left of the item.

1. _____ Running out into oncoming traffic on the street.
2. _____ Bedtime
3. _____ Time and circumstances of dating
4. _____ Underage drinking
5. _____ Coming in from playing outside
6. _____ Trying out for a team sport
7. _____ Being friends with the children of your parents' friends
8. _____ Taking a job
9. _____ Pulling an all-nighter to study for an exam
10. _____ Driving and abiding by the rules of the road
11. _____ Sexual Identity
12. _____ Waking up after being put to bed and coming to sleep the rest of the night with you

13. _____ Waking up after being put to bed and coming into your room for snuggle time

14. _____ Attending church

15. _____ Computer gaming time

On review of the above fifteen items, notice that age and circumstance can influence whether an item is a boundary or a choice. Go back over each item and mark to the right at what age you might negotiate with your child about the item.

Entitlement vs. the Common Good

Talk to any grandparent or great grandparent, and they will tell you about how it was "back in the day." Then, children were seen but not heard, and they minded their parents out of fear of being beaten. Thankfully, we are not living back in the day now. Children were considered more property than people and families contended more with physical and sexual child abuse.

The depression of the 1930's created hard times for all of America. Children were forced to grow up too fast, given adult responsibilities and jobs so that families could eat, and their childhoods were lost. World War II brought more heartache, but also economic relief. With the return home of our soldiers, the baby boomer generation was born. The opulence of the fifties spelled relief for the depression and war generations. The anti-war sentiment and civil rights/social changes of the sixties and seventies, followed by more economic boom, fueled by the information technology of the eighties and nineties, all paved the way for a sense of individuality and entitlement among the children and grandchildren of baby boomers.

Entitlement refers to the individual sense children have that they "should" get what they want. There is no sense of earned privilege. There is expectation that needs and wants will be met without work or effort on their part. This mindset spawns the "me generation." That is, what's in it for me? Cater to me. What I want and need is all that matters to me.

While it is a blessing when families have the resources to provide for more than the basic food, clothing, shelter needs of children, it is a curse when a sense of entitlement pervades the family mentality. Left unabated, parents are led to believe that they are bad parents if their children don't have all the latest gadgets and if they don't come and go as they please. While servanthood is a goal of effective parenting, servanthood is not Christ-like when it is the result of the children's sense of entitlement.

The antidote to a sense of entitlement in families is promoting the common good. Parents can promote the common good in their families by understanding the feelings, needs, wants, and expectations of each child and each other. Those are the ingredients in the pot. Then the pot is stirred by asking such questions as,

How does your perspective impact the rest of us?

Do you get what you want at our expense?

How does this promote your growth toward responsible independence?

What can we do that benefits all of us?

What can we do that increases our sense of family-ness?

Answers to these questions promote the common good. They define effective parenting. They help children realize that they are part of a whole, a piece in the puzzle of life. Frequent check-in time, what I call "How was your day, dear?" time, a monthly family event calendar, joint awareness of the family budget, and check-off, daily chore lists all provide tangible evidence of the family promoting the common good. Periodic family meetings allow for mid-course corrections and keep the dialogue current among family members. As issues come up, keep the common good questions in mind while problem-solving.

Learning the Concept: Exercise 10, Boundaries Exercise—Family Rules

As a family, take time to talk together about role and boundary expectations. First, list the 10 most important rules by which your family operates. Put these rules in the form of positive behavior. For example, "no hitting one another" becomes "play nicely together." Do the "no" list first and then get creative in finding ways to convert the "no" message into a positive reference. "Positively no hitting" doesn't count!

FAMILY RULES LIST

1.
2.
3.
4.
5.
6.
7.
8.
9.
10.

Second, now talk as a family about your respective family job descriptions. In a family, the jobs include father, mother, son, daughter, brother, and sister. Use a typical job description format complete with:

1. Objective in completing this job effectively.
2. Qualifications or training you have had to master this job.
3. Ways you are expected to conduct yourself at home, school, job, in private, or in public.
4. Goals or outcomes expected in your successful completion of this job.

Finally, create a two decorative posters, one for the family rules and one of all the job descriptions for display in your home.

Allowing for Individuality Without Entitlement

In Scripture, Jesus taught a lesson using the parable of the Prodigal Son (Luke 15: 11-28). This is a favorite Bible reference for Sunday School teachers and pastors because so many life lessons can be taught from it. A man had some wealth and two sons. All worked in the fields and supervised the field hands in processing the livestock and crops. When the younger son came of age (probably around age 15 in Bible times), he went to his father and demanded his half of the family inheritance right then. He wasn't content to get his inheritance after the father died.

The father could have justifiably said no to this son, fearing the worst. He could have felt obligated to give both sons their equal inheritance, so as to be fair. He could have given the elder son his inheritance, but not the younger son, because the elder son worked harder in the fields and showed more adult maturity and responsibility. The father did none of these options.

Rather, Jesus taught, the father acceded to his younger son's demand. Straightaway, the boy took off to foreign lands and a life of fun and reckless abandon. However, after his fortune had run out and he tired of honest work, the younger son came home. He fully expected to be disowned, scolded, and turned away as punishment for abandoning his responsibilities and squandering his fortune. He decided to beg his father to simply hire him as a lowly field hand.

Instead, the father, who had grieved daily for his long lost son, saw him in the distance and rushed to greet him. He treated him like royalty, without a hint of disappointment, anger, or betrayal. Only the fattest lamb for the homecoming feast, the finest silken robe, leather sandals, and, oh yes, the family signet ring for his prodigal son.

Is this a story of entitlement or individuality? The answer is both. The prodigal son had worked dutifully for his father until coming of age, and then he asked for his portion of the family pot. He could be seen as selfish or entitled, as irresponsible or individual. His father could have declined his request. He could be seen as justified, because of the needs of the business or as protective, as wise, or as withholding.

Add the elder brother to the mix and the story takes on other dimensions. On his brother's return, seemingly years later, the older sibling felt slighted by their father. The one who "messed up" gets a lavish party and full pardon? What's with that? So angry is the older brother that he refuses to celebrate the homecoming. His rage about feeling neglected and unappreciated for all his hard work over the years leads to his choosing to be left out of the homecoming. The father empathizes and explains, "My son, you have been with me always. But your brother, who was dead, is alive and home."(Luke 15:32)

Abiding Love Guides Parental Decisions

In healthy families, ultimately, parental decisions are not driven by issues of entitlement nor individuality, but by an abiding love. Had the father of the prodigal son denied his request for practical reasons, the emotional distance between him and his son would have widened. While he might have been justified to accept his son back as only a lowly laborer, because he "owed" him, the same emotional chasm would have resulted. Instead, the father showed unconditional, abiding love. The emotional bond, even if it feels one way at times, is more important to the health of all family members than pride or "being right."

Ultimately, in parenting, there are few absolute, right decisions. Where safety is paramount, such as blocking a toddler from harm's way, right decisions are absolute, even if they are unpopular. For the most part, especially as children reach adolescence and then begin to think abstractly, the advising parent practices abiding love for each individual child and balances issues of entitlement against the common good and our ultimate parental goal of launching independent, responsible adults. Every parent has defended the accusation from their child that you love her sibling more/better than her. Abiding love negates this challenge.

During play therapy where intense sibling rivalry is problematic in a family, I will occasionally read a children's book with my patient, entitled, If It Weren't For Benjamin (Hazen, 1983)). The younger sibling is left out of a trip to a baseball game and offers this as proof to his dad that he loves Benjamin more than him. The dad wisely reminds his younger son that he takes Benjamin to ball games because he loves sports. He takes the younger son to the zoo and to concerts because he loves animals and music.

Abiding parental love embraces the differences in our children, as evidence of God's gift of temperamental individuality. To the proverbial and inevitable question, we can answer honestly, "I love each of you with an abiding and complete love, and express it to you individually in special and unique ways." Isn't that just how Jesus loves us?

Tough Love is Also Abiding

James Dobson, in his groundbreaking classic, The Strong-Willed Child (1976) originated the term "tough love." The term gives reason to parental actions that seem, at first blush, unloving of your child. In reality, they are very loving, as they teach children about life in the real world. They represent a short-term loss for a long-term gain. Oftentimes, strategic tough love accomplishes a profound one-trial learning experience for your child.

For example, Dr. James Faye, author of <u>Love and Logic</u> (2006), tells the story of a third grader whose parents consulted him about their son's chronic tardiness from school. Their morning routine involved much coaxing, cajoling, promising reward if he would only get up on time for breakfast and to catch the school bus. His mother repeatedly drove him to school anywhere from minutes to hours late, after finally completing the morning routine.

After surveying the circumstances and extracting commitment from the parents to explicitly follow through with his intervention, Dr. Faye simply told the parents to abide by the bus schedule and get their son on the school bus at the required time, regardless of his state of readiness. Of course, he cleared the intervention with the bus driver and the boy's teacher and principal before the fateful morning.

Mom got the boy up on time and reminded him of what he had to do to be ready for the school bus. She told him that she had fixed him his favorite breakfast. The clothes he had picked out the night before had been neatly laid out for him. As had been the case for mornings on end before, the boy promptly fell back asleep.

Subsequently, when the school bus arrived at the appointed time, the boy's dad picked him up out of bed, still in his pajamas, and delivered him to the school bus. He awoke and protested loudly, as the children laughed at his attire and the bus driver pulled away. The principal met his bus at school and ushered him into his office to change into the clothes his parents had provided for the day. His tummy rumbled throughout the morning, as he missed his breakfast. However, from that day on, he never missed breakfast or the bus again.

God's Tough Love

After Cain killed Abel, God exacted tough love with him. In Genesis 4:5-8, the story is recorded: The Lord said to Cain,

"What's wrong with you? Why do you have such an angry look on your face? If you had done the right thing, you would be smiling. But you did the wrong thing, and now sin is waiting to attack you like a lion. Sin wants to destroy you, but don't let it."

And then in Genesis 4:19,23, Cain responds:

"Then the Lord said, "Why have you done this terrible thing? You killed your own brother, and his blood flowed onto the ground. Now his blood is calling out for me to punish you…" "This punishment is too hard!" Cain said, "You are making me leave my home and live far from you. I will have to wander about without a home, and just anyone could kill me."

While God portrayed tough love with his child, Cain, in the banishment, he also conveyed abiding love. After hearing Cain's plea, God added the condition that Cain would have a mark, a sign from God, which would protect him from harm. While he remained banished, shunned by others, the mark kept him alive. He was outcast, but not dead. He did more for Cain than Cain had done for Abel. Tough love, in any measure, is helping your children accept the natural consequences of their behavior.

The Toughest Abiding Love—
The Nurturing-Holding Procedure

Unfortunately, parents of extremely unruly children must set physical limits commensurate with the extreme circumstances. Their abiding love for their child calls for use of the Nurturing-Holding Procedure (NHP). The NHP is a means of physically containing and controlling your child when he/she is out of control (See Appendix 5).

The child is breaking objects, physically attacking you or others, screaming, flailing, in great danger of hurting himself or others. You must protect him, your property, your loved ones, and yourself.

Before executing the NHP, prompt your child as to what to expect. Keep your voice modulated, soft, and reassuring. Say what you are going to do, and then do it. For example, you might say, "Joey, get yourself together now. You're out of control. Take a breath, step back, and calm down. If you are not going to, or can't control yourself now, then I love you enough to do it for you. If I need to hold on to you to help you get yourself back in control, then I will, but only for as long as you need me to."

Positioning is essential. Depending on your size and that of your child, stand, sit, or lay down behind him. Wrap your legs around his legs and your arms around his body, pressing his arms to his side or holding his arms across his body. Pull your head back from his head, so that you won't get head-butted. Slide your hands to his waist or lower chest, so you won't get bitten. Tightly and properly executed, your child will be secure, immobile, and safe.

Children being controlled by use of the NHP will fight it. They will try to wrestle out of your hold. They will curse and scream in your ear. The more firm, and yet quieter and softer you are, the quicker your child will calm down. You model the calm you want them to achieve. To their fury you offer reassurance, "It's okay, Joey. I love you and I won't let you go until you are back in control. I love you so much that I will control you and keep you safe until you can control yourself." As he shows the slightest let-up, identify it and reinforce it, such as, "Okay, you're a little calmer. I can tell that you are beginning to get control back."

My experience with patients in my office, as their parents watch with grave concern, is that even the most tenacious children have trouble maintaining resistance and out of control behavior for much more than twenty minutes while I apply the NHP. Sometimes children will accede and then go limp. They will thank you for helping them get control back. You release your control and then they run amok once again. If this worst case scenario happens, simply catch them and re-apply the NHP with the observation, "Okay then, I guess you weren't really ready to calm down yet. I won't control you any longer than you need me to, but you need to get back in control of yourself."

Thankfully, the NHP is an extreme parenting tool used only in extreme circumstances. The focus is not on being bigger or stronger than your child. Rather, it is on loving him even when he does not show love for you or for himself. It is a reluctant tool that reinforces firm limits and abiding, tough love.

Learning the Concept: Effectively Using the Nurturing-Holding Procedure (NLP)

Appendix 5 gives rationale, procedure, and expected outcome of using the NLP for parents whose children so consistently and physically destroy boundaries that they put themselves and others in danger. Although there are mental health conditions that can generate extreme out-of-control behavior that the child cannot help, these occurrences are rare. Mostly, "wild children" are immature, consistently testing the limits, and expect to get what they want when they want it. The NLP is a physical, therapeutic procedure designed to lovingly aid your child in his getting his personal control back. When a child has personal control, neither he nor those around him are in danger of being physically injured, and established boundaries are upheld.

Talk with each other about whether and how the NLP can be used in your family.

Boundaries, Punishment, and Natural Consequences

One way that parents demonstrate abiding love is by securing boundaries and limits for your children. What about when boundaries are violated, and limits are tested?

A classic research experiment in developmental child psychology put toddlers in the center of a large room with toys and play objects lining each wall of the room. When they were shown the room without their parent, the toddlers dashed to a wall and began playing with the toys. When their parent accompanied them to the room and stood in the center with them, they hesitated in their exploration. Even with encouragement by the parent, the toddlers consistently looked over their shoulder to check in with the parent even as they played. Even toddlers feel safer, more secure, when the boundaries are affirmed by the parent.

Children also, for the most part, know when they are about to do something wrong or "against the rules." Tell your child "No," or, "Don't touch that," and what happens? Automatically they reach for the forbidden object, with a glance toward you as if to challenge, "What are you going to do about it?" As parents, we must accept this challenge and do something about it.

The Bowers Re-Visited

Even cute, little Gracie messes up occasionally. One day, after Emily had picked her little sister up from her after-school program, she noticed that Grace was wearing an expensive, new wristwatch. She questioned her about the watch. It was Grace's birthday and she had come home from school with several gifts from classmates. Grace said that her boyfriend, Mark, had given the watch to her. Emily was suspicious because this gift was no toy. She told their mom after Lauren had gotten home. Lauren questioned Grace fully, giving her opportunity to "fess up," but Grace stuck to her story.

The next day, Lauren took Grace to school and walked with her to class. She asked Grace's teacher about the gift from Mark and, to Lauren's horror, the teacher identified the watch as her own. She explained that she had thought she had misplaced it the other day and had been scouring the classroom and her home for it since then. Grace was nailed. The watch was returned to its rightful owner.

Lauren and Jim talked over lunch that day about how to handle Grace's theft and lying. When Grace got home that afternoon, her parents were waiting for her. They explained the crime, its ramifications, and her consequences. Grace had hoped the misadventure was over when the watch had been returned to her teacher. Jim and Lauren, however, talked at length with her about the natural consequences of her actions. They informed her that she was to write letters of apology to Mark, for involving him in her crime, and to her teacher, as victim of her crime. They also had her research the terms, theft and lying, and then write a three page paper explaining how those terms applied to her actions. After the paper was complete and given to her parents, Grace got a visit from a local police officer, at her parents' request, who expanded her awareness of the greater possible consequences to her actions. Grace never stole anything again.

Punishment vs. Natural Consequences

Other parents might have grounded Grace, had her do yard work, or spanked her for her misdeeds. These are examples of punishment. By definition, punishment is hard, hurts, and swift. It is also mostly ineffective in terms of long-term impact on the child. The Bowers, on the other hand, identified their daughter's misdeeds as a teachable moment and followed it with their natural consequences.

Punishment helps you express your rage, disappointment, and embarrassment as a result of your child's poor choices. Punishment makes you feel better, like you did something about the situation, at the expense of your child. In the extreme, punishment leads to physical abuse. Punishment is about you, not about your child. It also frequently leads to your child's lower sense of self-worth, and emotional distance from you. With repeated punishment, children frequently disconnect the crime from the punishment. There is no lesson learned, and so the misdeeds are repeated or expanded.

Natural consequence, on the other hand, provides your child with an opportunity to learn from their mistakes, put the misdeeds in context, and to understand the spread of effect resulting from their errors. Natural consequence is about your child. In Scripture, Paul acknowledged, "All have sinned and fallen short of the glory of God." (Rom 3:23) Natural consequence accepts this reality and moves on. There is no long-term lessening of your child's self-worth. Emotional bonding with you is secure. Your child continues to connect crime and consequence, learning the lesson in order to make better choices.

While punishment offers a challenge to your child, to see just how secure those limits are, natural consequences provide a map of their environment and their social exchange, so that they know precisely where the boundaries are and how they are to act.

Children need firm limits to their behavior. It helps them identify who they are. It encourages healthy interaction with their environment. It promotes their making good choices. It is evidence of your abiding love for your children. In abiding love, you are able to balance individuality with entitlement. You encourage the common good of the family. You provide direction and emotional stability for your children by using their inevitable limit-testing misdeeds as teachable moments. Natural consequences teach far more to children than punishment ever will.

Learning the Concept: Exercise 11, Punishment vs. Natural Consequences

When children need to be disciplined, we have the option to punish them in accordance to their "crime." Alternatively, we have the option to affect natural consequences. Punishment typically generates more clever criminals, while natural consequences provide your child with a teachable moment and an opportunity to learn from and correct their mistake.

Review the list below. Put a **P** next to items that are a **Punishment**. Put an **NC** next to items that are a **Natural Consequence**.

1. _____ Fifty push-ups
2. _____ Moving a dirt pile
3. _____ Writing a letter of apology
4. _____ Paying money into a "curse word" jar
5. _____ Writing sentences 500 times
6. _____ Looking up references/definitions of missing attributes or virtues (such as honesty, friendship, etc.) and writing a 3-page essay on it
7. _____ Taking shoplifted merchandise back to the store and giving it to the store manager
8. _____ Putting together a power point presentation on why a bad habit needs to be corrected (e.g., smoking, drinking alcohol, doing drugs)
9. _____ Confinement, grounding, or loss of privileges for a specified length of time
10. _____ Writing a 5-page paper on how the loss of privileges is related to the crime and what you will do to regain your privileges.
11. _____ Losing a job for being chronically late to work
12. _____ Restricting computer gaming time
13. _____ Replacing "homework" time with "study time" after receiving a failing grade
14. _____ Ten spanks for lying
15. _____ Washing your child's mouth out with soap for cussing

Now, have a family meeting to discuss your answers to the above exercise. Provide rationale for the family as to why you saw some items as punishment and others as natural consequence. Talk about the benefits and liabilities of each. Come up with your own family list of punishments and natural consequences.

Family List of Punishments and/or Natural Consequences

1.
2.
3.
4.
5.
6.
7.
8.
9.
10.

SUMMARY

Again, children test the limits of an environment to be sure that the limits are there. The most loveless thing you can do for your child is to allow him to be in charge, run wild, and be the boss. This freedom says to the child, "I don't care what you do. I have neither love nor responsibility for you. Grow yourself up." On the other hand, healthy boundaries, negotiated as children become teens, say to the child, "I love you so much that I will protect you from harm even if you can't see it. I will guide your steps and teach you to love one another as you love yourself. I will make sense of life for you until you can make sense of it for yourself."

You do not win popularity or friendship contests with your children by securing responsible boundaries for them. You do, however, demonstrate love, respect, and responsibility, and will teach your children to express these core values in return. Good boundaries express abiding love.

Lord, you are the author and example of abiding love. Help my children see through me your abiding love for all of us. Help me resist the temptation to be only the popular parent or friend to my child, when what they want from me is instruction, guidance, advice, and wisdom. I know that your gift of parenting is about my children, and not about me. I accept your confidence in me to train them up in the ways of the Lord. I know that "I hate you" from my child is temporary, but your love abides forever. Give me strength to show your abiding love through securing firm, responsible limits for my children at each stage of their journey to adulthood. Amen.

Chapter Four

Children Never Mean
What They Say

A child's world is not the real world. At least it's not our world. They live in the world of possibilities, fantasy, and accommodation. As infants and toddlers, of necessity and by nature, children are self-oriented and need-based. As their parents, we help children fit into the greater world of family, community, and society.

A first step on that journey is to be privileged to enter their world. We are better equipped for this journey if we have a map and know the language. With these tools, we will be able to debrief our children on expectations of the real world. We will also be able to decode what they say to better understand how they feel and what their words mean. As guides, we can help our children traverse the pitfalls of their world and, by the time they reach adulthood, help them make the transition and embrace the expectations of the real world.

Use the Map—Developmental Ages and Stages

Two early pioneers of developmental psychology still hold sway today on understanding the world of children and teens. Erik Erikson (1994) theorized eight stages of psychosocial development. From his unique perspective, children are faced with choice points in their development. Their choices are the product of life circumstances, parenting decisions, and the impact of psychosocial stressors on their lives. At its core, Erikson postulates that children make these choices by these ages:

By age 2, children learn trust or mistrust for their family and environment. With trust, they become secure and optimistic. The goal of this stage completion is hope.

By age 4, children learn autonomy or shame. With autonomy, they become proud, in bodily control, and they maintain high self-esteem. The goal of this stage completion is developing a will.

By age 6, children learn initiative or guilt. With initiative, they are imaginative and cooperative. The goal of this stage completion is purpose.

By age 12, children learn industry or inferiority. With industry, they are self-disciplined. They have positive peer relations. They work toward a common good. The goal of this stage completion is competence.

By age 20, teens learn identity or diffusion. With identity, they are more self confident, individualized, and they value achievement. The goal of this stage completion is fidelity.

By age 30, adults learn intimacy or isolation. With intimacy, they have a capacity to love. The goal of this stage completion is meaningful connection with another.

By age 60, adults learn generativity or self-absorption. With generativity, their capacity to care deeply increases. They feel accomplished in work and family. They feel creative and self-expansive. The goal of this stage completion is productivity.

Beyond age 60, adults learn integrity or despair. With integrity, they are more realistic and have an abiding faith in self (and in God). They feel fulfilled. The goal of this stage completion is wisdom.

As children (and adults) navigate these choice points, their reaction to life experiences becomes more positive or negative. Successful navigation of earlier stages encourages success through subsequent stages. Your awareness of these ages and stages helps you promote your child's positive journey.

Similarly, Arnold Gesell (in Ilg, Bates, & Baker, 1992) undertook a lifetime of longitudinal research on the ages and stages of cyclical changes in our children's temperament. Knowing where your child is in his changing emotional intensity better equips you to parent him through the current crisis. It also helps your child make some sense of the craziness he's feeling and soothes his fears that something is terribly wrong with him.

By following a core of fifty children over the course of their first twenty-five years of life, Gesell and his researchers concluded that children:

At ages 1, 5, and 10 are for the most part sunny and serene.
At ages 2, 6, and 11, children are typically loving, but can be defiant.
At ages 3, 7, and 12, children go through phases of being sullen.
At ages 4, 8, and 13, children often are lively and outgoing.
At ages 9 and 14, children become thoughtful, but can be mysterious.

Together, these psychosocial stages of development and cyclical periods of temperament provide the map that you can share with your children to help you and them make sense of their current life circumstances. While these are fluid dynamics of child development, they offer general guidelines that will help your children feel that you understand what they're going through.

Learning the Concept: Exercise 12, Developmental Ages and Stages

Following is a list of the stages of psychosocial development, as outlined by Erik Erikson (1994). For each stage, list 5 behaviors or situations that you can imagine children experiencing. List 5 for each side of the developmental equation.

By age 2, children learn to trust as demonstrated by

1.

2.

3.

4.

5.

Or, they learn to mistrust as demonstrated by

1.

2.

3.

4.

5.

By age 4, children learn autonomy as demonstrated by

1.

2.

3.

4.

5.

Or, they learn shame as demonstrated by

1.

2.

3.

4.

5.

By age 6, children learn initiative as demonstrated by

1.

2.

3.

4.

5.

Or, they learn guilt as demonstrated by

1.

2.

3.

4.

5.

By age 12, children learn industry as demonstrated by

1.

2.

3.

4.

5.

Or, they learn inferiority as demonstrated by

1.

2.

3.

4.

5.

By age 20, teens learn identity as demonstrated by

1.

2.

3.

4.

5.

Or, they're identity is diffused as demonstrated by

1.

2.

3.

4.

5.

By age 30, adults learn intimacy as demonstrated by

1.

2.

3.

4.

5.

Or, they learn isolation as demonstrated by

1.

2.

3.

4.

5.

By age 60, adults learn generativity as demonstrated by

1.

2.

3.

4.

5.

Or, they learn self-absorption as demonstrated by

1.

2.

3.

4.

5.

Beyond age 60, adults learn integrity as demonstrated by

1.

2.

3.

4.

5.

Or, they learn despair as demonstrated by

1.

2.

3.

4.

5.

Jason's Adolescent Angst

Jim noticed a relative calm in the home after he and Jason returned from the local public library. Emily was sitting on the couch, buried in a novel she was reading for her senior lit class. Lauren was at the computer in the kitchen catching up on her e-mails. Gracie had long conked out in her bed. After putting his coat in the hall closet, he turned to Jason and suggested, "Hey, Son. Why don't you take some time to look through your reference books from the library while it's fresh on your mind?"

"Huh?" Jason mumbled, as he shuffled past, slowly ascending the stairs to his bedroom.

"You know, I'm just thinking you could attack this project." Jim paused and then continued thinking out loud, "It's just, well, you have your commentaries now. Why don't you at least check out how they can help you with the book report?"

"Yeah, whatever," Jason replied as he continued trudging up the stairs.

"Jason, stop for a minute." His son stopped his trek and released a slow, exaggerated sigh.

Jim paused to gather his thoughts. "I don't understand you, Son. You made such a fuss about not having these books from the library. You expected your sister to drop everything and take you there immediately. And now you're blowing it off? What's with that?"

"With what?" Jason glazed over as he responded.

"Hellooo. Earth to Jason, Come in, Jason."

"Leave me alone, Dad."

Jim decided to take another tack. "I'm sorry, Son," he softened. "I didn't mean to make fun of you. I just don't understand what's more pressing than cranking out this book report while it's on your mind?"

Jason looked away and rolled his eyes. "Dad, the book report isn't due until next Tuesday."

"So why make such a fuss tonight to go to the library?"

"I dunno."

"What's so important that you can't get a jump start on the report?"

"Nothing. Anything." Jason took another exaggerated breath and then looked at his watch. "Dad, Allison is expecting me to call her at 9:30. Do you mind?"

Jim threw his hands up and shook his head in not-too-well-hidden disgust. He then turned to find his wife.

At 15, Jason is smack in the middle of the <u>sturm</u> <u>und</u> <u>drang</u>, storm and stress, of adolescence. His very core is quivering with indecision, internal demands to conform or rebel, and with choices about what's right or what he wants. In Erikson's stage format, Jason is wrestling with formulating a personal identity. His decisions and life circumstances will gently nudge him either toward identity integration or further into the morass of identity diffusion.

Add to the mix that Jason's cycle of temperament is coming out of the thoughtful but mysterious phase, according to Gesell's research. He is full of tension, worry, and distance at age 15. Such temperament is destined to strain relationships and increase isolation. Teens tend to bond with kindred spirit, mold into cliques or gangs, and seek out first love relationships for this very reason. They seek unspoken understanding as a salve to their psychic and spiritual unrest.

At 42, Jim is developing generativity in his stage of life. His income is secure. His relationships are rewarding. He is stretching his boundaries to explore possibilities beyond the routine. In contrast to his son, Jim has been there, done that. He could fall into the trap of making Jason conform, because he knows what the outcome of his son's choices will be.

However, because adolescent angst and rebellion is a required rite of passage into adulthood, if Jim were to strong-arm his son, he would only be delaying the inevitable, and perhaps at a higher cost to his son. Also, Jim can identify with Jason's restlessness, as he tries to find balance in middle age. Both he and Jason are confused, yet passionate about experiencing life, because of the cyclical nature of temperament.

Know the Language—Decoding Words and Actions

While the outcome was not what Jim wanted, he did hang in there with his son. When teens act clueless, it is frequently because they are. Jim's well-intentioned advice to Jason fell on deaf ears for the moment. Sometimes, the best parents can do is prompt, plant seeds, and wait. When our teens fall, we catch them and help them through the natural consequences of their actions.

Decoding what our children and teens mean by their words, and understanding the underlying feelings, is the heart of relational bonding and effective parenting. For example, the following is a list of common phrases that Jason used with his dad, along with their possible decoded meaning:

Huh?—You startled me out of my internal world.

Yeah, whatever.—How lame can you be? Or, I don't want to talk about it.

With what? —If I confuse you, maybe you will go away.

Leave me alone.—Now I know that you are right, but I won't tell you that.

I dunno.—I don't want to talk about it. Or, I really don't know the answer.

Nothing. Anything.—I'm not telling you. I'm really confused. Okay, I'll tell you (Allison phone call), but I know you'll be really mad (dad throws hands up and walks off). I knew you'd act that way. Oh, well.

Children and teens rarely mean what they say. To borrow a phrase from the treatment of alcohol and other addictive disorders, believe everything children do and nothing they say. While this feels harsh, it is wiser to err on the side of caution. With healthy, effective parenting, children's words and actions will match up often.

When you observe consistent, difficult behavior from your child, and you want to get a discussion going with him about the behavior, consider this incisive question:

"Jason, this really isn't like you at all. What else is going on here?"

With this question, you are offering your child a left-handed complement. If fact, you are saying, "this isn't how I want you to be," and you are promoting his capacity to change. The question, "What else is going on?" encourages a cognitive search, which engages your child in a joint problem-solving venture with you.

Frequently, younger children, and recalcitrant teens, don't answer essay questions very well. If you get the ever-present shoulder shrug to your essay question, make it a multiple choice question, based on your knowledge of recent events in his life. Almost always your child will register, usually nonverbally, with one of your choices.

Decoding is a full-time parenting task, especially when helping your child through a difficulty or when he is struggling to understand himself. Jim did not hang in there with Jason, but he could come back to the exchange later. Teachable moments are never lost. They can be recaptured later, when your child is less distracted by pressing things.

When Jim apologized to Jason for his flip comment, he set the groundwork for getting to the heart of the concern if not at that moment, then later. Kids frequently give up on understanding something or working through feelings. Healthy parents never give up on trying to understand their children and helping them understand themselves.

Learning the Concept: Exercise 13, Know the Language— Decoding words and actions

Children rarely mean what they say. They have coded words and actions that determine whether or not they will let you in their world. Nowadays, in addition to colloquialisms, private speech, gestures, and teenage jargon, we parents also have to contend with computer speak. Such short-hand is preferred communication in texting, in chat rooms on line, on MySpace and Twitter, and even among many bloggers and twitters.

Keeping up with the changes in communication among young people lets them know you are interested in what they have to say. You bridge the generation gap and get a certain measure of "cool."

Review the following list of words, phrases, and actions with your children or other children/teens. Find out what each item means in adult-speak. Write the possible decoding or definition to the right of the item.

1. "Whatever"
2. "Dude"

3. "LOL"
4. "Huh?"
5. Shoulder shrug
6. Rolling of the eyes
7. "I L B L8"
8. Eye contact
9. "Whoa"
10. Playing with a toy while you are talking to him
11. Touching your hand
12. Walking behind (or ahead of) you in the mall
13. "Totally!"
14. Zoned into computer gaming
15. Looking at you while doing the exact thing you are telling him not to do

Now, ask each family member to come up with as many other computer-speak, chat room, my space, Facebook words and phrases you can think of or research. Each of you write a list of your 10 favorite, most accurate, or most descriptive phrases. Share your lists and research with each other and compile a family dictionary of abbreviated words and phrases. You can have so much fun with this exercise that you might LOL yourself!

Finally, talk about the behaviors and mannerisms of each family member and what each means to you. For example, when I put the newspaper up in front of me and begin to read it, my behavior signals "Leave me alone. This is my reading time." What do you suppose it means when your teen rolls her eyes at you? When your son isolates in his room for hours at a time? When your mom doesn't pick you up at the appointed, agreed upon time? What other behaviors or mannerisms can you think of that are relevant for your family?

Paul's Admonition in Scripture

The Apostle Paul had plenty to say to the church in Ephesus, a trading crossroad in Asia Minor (modern day Turkey) and the epicenter of pagan worship. His preaching created a groundswell of local support for this new religion called Christianity. Sadly, though, even the church elders could not sustain the intense fervor of Paul's passionate faith in Jesus Christ after Paul left town to continue his missionary work throughout the region. After getting word of disintegrating circumstances within his planted church in Ephesus, Paul wrote back. His letters became Ephesians in the Bible. Chapters 4 and 5 echo my conviction that children never mean what they say, and Paul offers a salve for this malady:

> "We are part of the same body. Stop lying and start telling each other the truth. Don't get so angry that you sin. Don't go to bed angry, and don't give the devil a chance. If you are a thief, quit stealing. Be honest and work hard, so you will have something to give to people in need. Stop all your dirty talk. Say the right thing at the right time and help others by what you say. Don't make God's Spirit sad. The Spirit makes you sure that someday you will be free from your sins. Stop being bitter and angry and mad at others. Don't yell at one another or curse each other or ever be rude. Instead, be kind and merciful, and forgive others, just as God forgives you because of Christ. Do as God does. After all, you are his dear children. Let love be your guide." (Eph. 4:25–5:2)

Paul's admonition seems to follow naturally from the wisdom of Solomon in the Old Testament, when Solomon wrote:

> "Sharp words cut like a sword, but words of wisdom heal. Truth will last forever, lies are soon found out. An evil mind is deceitful, but gentle thoughts bring happiness." (Prov. 12:18-20)

SUMMARY

Children never mean what they say. A bit radical? Maybe. The intent is not to catch your child in lies. Rather, by recognizing that childspeak is a different language, we can accept the parenting challenge to help our children acclimate to the real world.

As we enter their world with the map of developmental stages and cycling of temperament, we will better understand their perspective on life circumstances. As they try to communicate with us using childspeak, we can continue to bond with them through active listening, keying in not only on understanding their words, but also their feelings. We then gain credibility to offer them a hand through their personal *sturm und drang* of life.

Lord, as I accept your gift of parenting my children in your ways, help me to speak the truth. Help me to get out of your way. Help me avoid sharp words that cut like a sword. Help me to say the right thing at the right time and help my children by what I say. Help me to be quick to listen, slow to speak, and slow to become angry. Help me be your instrument, and see through my eyes, hear through my ears, and feel through my heart. Give me opportunity to model kindness, mercy, and forgiveness for my children, just as You forgive me because of Christ. Thank you, God, for showing me how to let love be my parenting guide. Amen.

Chapter Five

A Family is Not a Democracy

S hould the family be democratic? Especially in our American culture, democratic themes abound. Our country was born to escape oppression. People have died, and still do, to preserve our democratic way of life. The principle of "one man, one vote" guides our political process. Especially in the aftermath of the 2000 presidential elections, where vice president Al Gore won the popular vote but lost the Electoral College vote to candidate George Bush, the importance of our democracy to our way of life has flourished. The family is the foundational building block of our society. Since we embrace democratic principles in our way of life, why should not families function democratically?

Imagine a Plexiglas, transparent pyramid that has layers you can see through. Above the pyramid is a cross with a bejeweled crown draped on it. This image captures both the nature and the strength of the family. Both the father and mother in a family sit atop the pyramid, reaching out and above in relationship with God. As that relationship individually is strong, nurturing, and personal with the Lord, so then are you able to love each other and nurture your marriage. As your marriage is nurtured and flourishes, so then do you have ample resources to love and give to your children. As your family thrives in God's grace and love, so then are you able to successfully go out beyond the family to your world of friends, work, and school. Each layer builds upon the strength of the higher one and deepens the integrity and intimacy of the pyramid structure. The pyramid would collapse if the family functioned as a democracy. The family is not a collection of equals. The strength emanates from above and infuses the structure with God's love and guiding principles.

In Ephesians 3: 15-17, Paul identifies the strength of the family, "All families in heaven and on earth receive their life from him. God is wonderful and glorious. I pray that his Spirit will make you become strong followers and that Christ will live in your hearts because of your faith. Stand firm and be deeply rooted in his love."

God charges you, as a couple, to love, guide, and care for your children. The strength of a family emanates from above and through you to your children. In I Corinthians 11: 11-12, Paul continues his explanation, "As far as the Lord is concerned, men and women need each other. It is true that the first woman came from a man, but all other men have been given birth by women. Yet God is the one who created everything." Again in Ephesians 5: 18, 21, Paul admonishes, "…be filled with the Spirit…submitting yourselves one to another in fear of God."

And to children and parents, in Ephesians 6:1-4, Paul captures the context of family, "Children, you belong to the Lord, and you do the right thing when you obey your parents. The first commandment with a promise says, 'Obey your father and your mother, and you will have a long and happy life.' Parents, don't be hard on your children. Raise them properly. Teach them and instruct them about the Lord."

Your children are God's children. You are His emissary to them. Proper raising and instruction of your children comes from God through you. If you are harsh with your children, that does not come from God. That comes from you, and you become a stumbling block for your children. Does that mean that your kids get their every heart's desire? Of course not. You consult with each other and with the Lord in prayer and in His Word, and then you make decisions designed to help your children draw nearer to the Lord.

The one man, one vote principle of democracy does not apply in the Christian family system. Ideally, where the decision affects all family members, husbands and wives consult one another, submitting to learn from each other's perspective, and decide jointly. If, after much prayer and discussion you don't come to an agreement as parents, then God calls the husband to decide, with all the love and devotion to the process that Christ showed for the church (Eph 5:22-33). Rather than a democracy, Christian families function similarly to a system run by a benevolent despot, where the ruler is a wise servant to his countrymen.

Loving your family as Christ loves the church is a tall order for any father. So often, we fall victim to power plays, pride, and ascribed authority, where our humanity bleeds through our intent. As we accept Christ's challenge to "pray unceasingly," we strengthen to the task of running the family. A brief prayer that I ask of God daily is simply, "Lord, please help me to get out of your way."

The Bower's Family Vacation

It was getting to be that time of year. School was winding down. The weather was warming. Spring had arrived and summer was around the corner. After settling into bed one night, Lauren and Jim shared their days with each other. They also talked about upcoming events in their own lives and in each of their children's lives. Ball schedules, recitals, school events, final exams all got dutifully noted. Their intimate conversation then turned to plans for summer vacation. How much money had they set aside? How much time from work could they afford? What vacation plans would seem to most fit the needs of the family and of each person in the family? After settling on their perspective, they agreed to call a family meeting. Sunday after church and during lunch would be a good time. Lauren planned a big lunch of everybody's favorite. If the weather cooperated, they would eat out on the back deck at the picnic table.

With several days' notice, the kids were able to accommodate their schedules and think about their contributions to the upcoming family meeting. Sunday came. They were able to convene on the deck. The meal was scrumptious and filling. As dessert was offered, Jim convened the family meeting.

"Okay, guys. Is everybody ready to tackle our vacation plans for this summer?"

"I'm not a guy, Daddy," Grace chimed in. "I'm a girl."

"And a very cute one at that," her daddy gushed as he tickled her side.

"Daddy, stoooop," Grace mock whined as she pushed her father's hand aside. Jason rolled his eyes with disdain.

Lauren scooped a bit of ice cream onto her slice of pecan pie. "Now children," She raised her eyebrow toward her husband as the words rolled off her tongue. Jim got the message and straightened up.

"Okay, guys," he began again, and then added pointedly, "and girls, let's make a wish list of vacation possibilities. Jason, would you please be the recorder for this meeting?"

"Aww, man. Do I hafta?" Jason grumbled.

"Well, let me see, uh, yes." Jim's hope was to keep his son active in the meeting by giving him something to do, so that he would more likely contribute. His sullenness at family meetings was legendary. "Just title the list, 'Vacation Options' and write down anything any one of us wants to put on the list," he added.

"That's brainstorming, right Daddy?" said his youngest daughter. Emily, on the other hand, looked at Grace and mouthed the words, suck up.

"Who wants to go first?" Lauren prompted. The following silence seemed forever.

"Well," Emily tentatively began, "If you don't mind, I'll pass on family vacation. After graduation, I was hoping to take a road trip to the West Coast with some of my friends."

"Emily, no," protested her mom. "It just wouldn't be..."

"Now, Lauren," her husband cut her off. "We're just brainstorming. Let them put possibilities on the list." Turning to his son, Jim directed, "Jason, just write that Emily opts out of being with the family for our two-week vacation." As Jason wrote it down, his dad continued, "Who else has ideas for our family?"

"If she's not going, then me neither," Jason grunted. He turned to his dad and awaited his challenge.

"Okay, Jason, write it down. Write 'me too.'

"Fine," Grace chimed in, "You guys be party poopers. I'm going to Disney World with mom and dad."

"That's a possibility." Jim noted, "Who else?"

"Wants to go to Disney World?" added Jason.

"No, we're not voting. Who else has other ideas?" clarified his dad. "Surely you all have some great, buried ideas in your brains. Think outside the box. If money and time were not a problem, and you could do anything you wanted to do, what would you choose?"

Lauren shifted her weight on the picnic bench. "I've always thought staying at a dude ranch out west would be fun."

Emily and Jason burst out laughing at the same time. Jason mimed roping a steer. "Yeehaw," he exclaimed in western drawl. "Ride 'em, cowboy."

Everyone laughed. Jim added, "Lauren, that certainly is an idea outside the box." He turned to the kids, "Come on, troops. I want at least fifteen possibilities."

The family meeting continued, and the Bower's came up with a list of twelve ideas, including white water rafting, renting a cabin by the lake, skydiving, two weeks at a condo at the beach, touring Europe, and cleaning out the garage (that one was Jim's). After a lull in voicing options, Jim shifted gears.

"Now, your mom and I have put aside money for our vacation and can take off two weeks in July. Given our time and money limitations, let's go back over this list and talk about why each item is on the list and whether the common family good will be served by that item. How realistic? How doable are these items as vacation plans for our family?"

Emily went into a defense of her road trip option, how she has saved for it, how it is a rite of passage from high school to college. Everyone listened intently, until she paused.

"I vote no on that one," Jason chimed in.

"Oh, yeah?" Emily started, "just wait until we get to one of your items on the list, buster."

"You could take mom and me with you," suggested Grace. "That way it would be a 'just girls' trip. Then I'd vote for it."

"Hold up, now, we're not voting," Jim clarified. "You mom and I want your input. We want to talk about how we each could benefit from our vacation and also how we would grow together as a family and in God's eyes."

"Not voting?" Jason added indignantly, "Then why are we talking. Just make the decision. You're gonna do what you want to do anyway."

"I'm sorry you feel that way, Son." Jim offered. "That's not my intention." He looked at his wife, and Lauren smiled back softly. "What we want is to understand all of the needs, wants, and feelings among us, and then talk it all out, all of us. If at all possible, we want each of us to come home from vacation this year and remember how terrific it was and what a great time we all had."

Emily shared a skeptical glance with her brother.

Lauren added, "This meeting is not the end of it. If we don't come to an understanding, we'll table the discussion until we can think more about it. We do need to be mindful, though, that rental places fill up fast. We might not get our first choice if we delay into May."

The meeting lasted about forty minutes. Every item on the list was explored and rationale offered. Particular attention was paid to needs and feelings, with Jim and Lauren noting when certain options seemed to address the needs and feelings of more than one person. As Jason and Emily had hit their stride socially, they were less inclined to defer to family time. Gracie, however, was up for anything. Jim and Lauren also offered their preferences and rationale as to how the options would meet their respective needs. Staying with the process, rather than jumping to solutions, was difficult. The kids, in particular, were used to getting answers and wanting their way. Jim concluded with prayer and asked God to touch each family member in the decision-making process, to help find the option that would make the family vacation the best ever.

Why Benevolent Despotism?

The Bower's family meeting captures the essence of benevolent despotism. Jim and Lauren are clearly the parents. They guide the meeting, support helpful comments, and also clarify and redirect unhelpful comments. Because of the differences in their developmental stages, each child brings a different perspective and agenda to the table. Gracie wants to please and tag along. Jason wants to be different and disruptive. Emily wants to move on to her next venue. In leading the meeting, Jim and Lauren continually refocus the kids to the meeting's purpose and reinforce that the kids have a say in the process but not in the decision. As parents, you gather your children's needs and feelings, expand them, get clarifying feedback, and move them at their pace toward an acceptance of the common good for all.

As children move toward a capacity for abstract thinking, along about age 12, many parents make the mistake of voting on matters of little consequence, while making uninformed decisions on big matters. This is a recipe for emotional distance, bitterness, and resentment for all family members. The hidden message behind voting on little matters is that the children's opinions are not that important, so we'll pretend we're democratic by "letting them win" some of the time. Children catch on to this hidden message quickly and feel slighted. At some point, parents then have to draw a line between what's voted on and what the parents decide. With the double standard exposed, many teens simply opt out of the process and retreat to their rooms, only to tolerate family time.

Also, when self-styled, "enlightened" parents promote a democratic approach to family decision-making, then parents can become outnumbered and, thus, outvoted. When kids are in charge, because they always test the limits in families, the result is often total anarchy. Parents yield the power differential and everybody loses. With a democratic approach to family, factions develop, lobbyists are born, and subgroups develop strategies to get the majority vote. Power struggles and manipulation become the rule of law in the family.

When you establish a system of benevolent despotism within the family, over time children are actually relieved. They feel more secure, safer, and become more vocal because they know their voices will be heard and good decisions will be made for them. The power differential is in place and a collective sigh of relief is palpable in the family.

Power Corrupts and Absolute Power Corrupts Absolutely

This conventional wisdom addresses the caution in a system of benevolent despotism. As parents, you retain all of the power to make individual and family decisions. If you focus on the despotism part of the system, you could fall victim to your own power. If the words, "I'm your father and you will do what I say" ever leave your mouth in mounting anger at your child, you have already lost that battle. The rationale "because I said so" never leads to effective conflict resolution. Your power in the family is ultimate, but it does not have to be absolute.

Power does not always corrupt. The adjective, benevolent, mitigates the corrupt potential of your despotism. In your benevolence, the process of decision-making and parenting becomes more important than the solutions. Your benevolence leads you to gather wisdom from your spouse and from your children before you decide. You focus on each person's needs and feelings, as well as on the impact of your decision for the common good of the family and its members.

The absolute power of God is not corruptible because he has a personal relationship with each of his children. He knows our needs and feelings. He is good in His grace, patient in His character. As parents to your children, when you heed the pop faith question, "What would Jesus do?" then your parenting will become inspired. As human beings, we all get stressed, have bad days, and are at times short-tempered. These are not good times for effective parenting. It's okay to occasionally tell your child, "not now. I need some me time. Get back to me later." Even Jesus made a habit of retreating to solitude after a busy day of teaching and healing. He recharged his batteries in prayer to the Father. We are his children too, and he is our role model in parenting our children. We pass his benevolence with us on to our children and avoid the pitfalls of power in parenting.

Learning the Concept: Exercise 14, Benevolent Despotism

Take a moment to define this term.

What is the scriptural admonition that Paul gives Christians, which is the Code of the Benevolent Despot? (Ephesians 3:17)

How would following this code effect, or change, your parenting style?

How powerful are you as a parent in your family? How is absolute power working for you?

Avoid the Parent Trap

After our first child was born, she developed colic. This is a 24/7 condition of stomach muscle contraction that results in incessant crying. After much angst, we set an appointment with a world renowned pediatrician. He spent five minutes with our baby and twenty-five minutes with us. His words still ring in my ears. "Your baby is one third of your family. She should have one-third of your time and attention."

While that sounds harsh, especially when your baby is so helpless and in pain, his intent was to help us avoid the parent trap.

In Amy Chua's book, The Battle Hymn of the Tiger Mother (2010), the author makes a case for going "all in" with your children. Demanding perfection and mastery, at all costs to you and to a balanced life, is worth it for your child to accomplish great things. Others bandy about the reference to "soccer moms." These parents seem to be at their child's beckened call, to shuttle them to soccer games and to all other functions. The hope here is to give your child a "well-rounded childhood," but also at all cost to you. Neither of these extremes provides the balance of activity and responsibility among all family members.

Charles and Elizabeth Schmitz, in their book, Building the Love that Lasts: The Seven Surprising Secrets of Successful Marriage (2008), found in a recent study of 218 couples that, over the first eight years of marriage, marital satisfaction dropped precipitously once couples became parents, compared to couples who had no children. The authors note, "The relationship between husband and wife should trump everything else. You have to keep it strong, keep the romantic energy. Everything else comes from that. Children are beautiful, but they're not the sole purpose of marriage."

When I work in couple therapy, I encourage the Me-You-Us approach to marriage and family. The Schmitz' refer to Time In, when you make time for each other. It can be as elaborate as a weekend getaway or a date night. It can also be as simple as going for a walk together. This is the "Us" time of your marriage. Time Out is also critical, which I call the "Me" and "You" time of your marriage. These are times of solitude, reflection of private thoughts, or simply time that you each take to get things done.

Finally, successful couples touch each other a lot. The touch can be sensual, or just intimate. It can be casual hand holding during a walk in the mall, or playful banter. These times acknowledge that your marriage is the source of your energy for the children and the family.

More specifically, reaching the goal of Christ-centered parenting for your children becomes easier to the extent that you re-charge your batteries daily, commit to personal and couple devotional time, and balance self-care with other-care.

Recharging Your Batteries Daily

You will make more good decisions for your children and maintain a higher level of Christ-centered, effective parenting as you are able to manage your own stress daily. In the process of recharging your batteries for optimal parenting, consider two resources:

Maintaining personal and couple devotional time, and balancing self-care with other-care.

Just as Jesus made a habit of getting away to himself, so too should we. We do this either physically or by reflection. Taking pause in your daily routine releases you from autopilot and helps you function purposefully. Such re-charging times help you move from "have-to's" to "want-to's" in life. Your perspective on routine tasks is changed, and you develop more passion for effective parenting.

Personal and Couple Devotional Time

Devotional time is planned, reflective activity. Typically, you set aside 15-30 minutes daily. Scripture calls us to pray "in our rising up, and in our laying down."(1 Thess. 5:17) Developing a personal devotional time first thing in the morning and last thing before going to bed helps you stay connected to God's will for your life. Devotional guides, such as The Upper Room (Upper Room Ministries, Inc.), or Open Windows (Life Way Christian Resources, Inc.) offer bits of wisdom and primes the pump for reflection. Devotional time also provides consistent opportunity to listen to God, using his wise counsel in addressing parenting concerns and other life stressors.

As a couple, devotional time is a shared experience of profound emotional and spiritual intimacy. Often this daily event occurs shortly before retiring. You may plan a personal devotional time early in the morning or other time in the day, while agreeing on your couple devotional time at bedtime. Many parents use this time as opportunity to check in with each other about the day's events, frustrations, as well as joys. Taking turns and active listening allow your full attention to your mate. After such spontaneous exchange, couples often then read out loud to each other from available couple devotional resources, such as Two-Part Harmony (1994) or Quiet Time for Couples (1990). Such guides stimulate discussion between you about couple or parenting topics that can enhance your relationships.

Learning the Concept: Exercise 15, Recharging Your Batteries Daily

With prayerful consideration, fill in the blanks of the following commitment statement:

From this day,_____, and forward, we commit to God and to ourselves to spend _____minutes in daily devotion. We will use _____ devotional guide, talk to each other about the application, and meditate on the attending prayer. We will do our daily devotion _____(approximate time of day and location)

_____(Husband)

_____(Wife)

Followers of Christ

Self-Care vs. Other-Care

During Jesus' ministry, certain Pharisees followed him from a distance. Some waited for opportunity to ask him genuine, thought provoking questions of faith. Others, however, asked questions only to trick Jesus into mis-stepping, and thus only seeking to discredit his ministry. On one such occasion, the Pharisees asked him, "Jesus, what is the greatest commandment?" (Matt. 22:36) They expected him to pick one of the Ten Commandments from Exodus. They could then find fault in his choice.

However, Jesus spoke two new commandments. He said, "The greatest commandment is to love your God with all your heart, mind, and soul. And the second greatest is to love one another as you love yourself." (Matt.22:39) This second greatest commandment is what has been referred to as the Codependent's Commandment.

Codependence defines a cluster of personality characteristics that cause you to care about others even at the expense of caring about yourself. Part of recharging your batteries as a healthy, Christ-centered parent involves balancing self-care with other-care.

Naturally, as parents you want the best for your children. You may go to extremes to care for them. As such, you are at risk for caring for your children and not caring for yourself. Super-parenting can be exhausting and, ultimately self-defeating. Jesus calls us to balance self-care with other-care, and thus avoid the pitfalls of super-parenting.

Many people avoid self-caring activity because they confuse self-care with selfish or self-interest. Being selfish or engaging in self-interest is activity based. Self-caring, on the other hand, is need based. Self-interest involves activity that has no consequence for others around you. Hobbies often fall into the self-interest category. Selfish involves activity that has specific, adverse consequences for others around you, and you persist regardless of those consequences. For example, scheduling your hobby at a time that your spouse is otherwise engaged and expecting you to pitch in for child care would turn a self-interest activity into a selfish activity.

Self-caring, on the other hand, is need based. It involves a filling up of your emotional void, satisfying your needs, and renewing your spirit. When your activity affects no one, then all that is required of you is to make time to fill yourself back up. When your activity does affect someone, then you find a way to get your self-care time and fulfill your obligations. With the example of a personal hobby, if the only time for your hobby conflicts with your spouse's schedule, then it would be self-caring for you to find alternative child care options, so that both yours and your spouse's needs could be met.

Too often as parents, we give up on ourselves. Whenever you care about others, your children and spouse, at the expense of caring about yourself, then there is a dear price for all to pay. The price is conditional loving. The exchange is, "I will do this for you, but you owe me. I won't even tell you that you owe me, and I won't tell you when I plan to collect."

Of course, the person being loved usually doesn't get the exchange, and so the debt is not fulfilled. Unfulfilled conditional loving leads to bitterness, resentment, and hostility in relationship. The imbalance in self-care and other-care is a lose/lose proposition that creates anger and emotional distance among family members.

As parents, we too often leave ourselves out of the equation. Other-care for our spouse and children far outweighs self-care. An imbalanced equation is a recipe for disaster and hardship in the family.

Learning the Concept: Exercise 16, The Context for Re-Energizing.

What is the difference between self-care, self-interest, and selfish?

Read Matthew 22:39. How does this qualify as the Codependents Commandment?

What is the typical outcome of conditional love, however well-intentioned?

What is the balance required to be able to give agape love?

List 5 self-care activities you can do daily to balance out self-care with other-care in your life.

1.

2.

3.

4.

5.

Agape Love—Outcome to Self-Care

When you make time for yourself, exercising self-care, you get to balance your self-care with the abundance of other-care you give your family. The result of a balance in self-care and other-care is agape love. In his commandment, Jesus calls us to love one another as we love ourselves. Following Jesus' commandment gives us the blessing of loving unconditionally. If you are "filled up" in terms of your own emotional resources, then you have plenty to give others from your abundance. You give because you can, and without condition. You move your family relationships from the "have to" category to the "want to" category.

Interestingly, this balance between self-care and other-care is not limited by time. By simply developing opportunity for incidental self-care, you recharge your batteries for abundant other-care. Defining self-care moments in your life provides you with the clear message to yourself: *I care. I matter to me. I can take care of my needs.* Just as Jesus went into the hills to pray in solitude occasionally, we too need to define moments in the day that recharge our batteries.

For example, I routinely set my clock for a half hour before I need to get up to go to work. This gives me the self-care opportunity to have a leisurely cup of coffee, read the paper, and do my devotional before beginning the daily grind. Additionally, I have a work-out routine that both helps me stay fit and also reduces my stress. Finally, I live five minutes from my office, so that I can come home for lunch each day, thereby breaking up the daily schedule and giving me something to look forward to in the middle of the day. Each of these activities is an example of time-limited self-care that re-charges my battery for the next expanse in my day.

SUMMARY

A family is not a democracy. It is a system of benevolent despotism. Through a process of gaining earned authority, and by taking into consideration the needs and feelings of all family members, as parents, you make all final decisions of import, or that have an impact on the common good of the family. As Paul encouraged, "Stand firm and be deeply rooted in his love." (Eph. 3:17) This is the code of the benevolent despot.

To succeed by this standard, you take into consideration the ages and stages of each family member. In a democracy, there can be voting factions, power plays, lobbying, and pork barrel riders that just appease your constituency. Benevolent despotism avoids these pitfalls. Family meetings are ideal for problem-solving and family plan making. As the benevolent despot, you demonstrate your fairness and your conviction that the process is more valuable than the solution.

To be an effective benevolent despot, you must balance self-care with other-care. When you take care of your own needs and feelings, you recharge your emotional resources and have more time and energy to care for the others in your family. Couple and personal devotional time also keep you plugged in to your ultimate energy source—God. Through God's grace and your hard work, you demonstrate his love in your family. His is an agape love, unconditional, abiding, and true.

Lord, help me learn from your example and be the effective, Christ-centered, benevolent despot to my family. Help me lead by example. Help me to avoid the pitfalls of being a friend, of being liked, by my children, at the expense of being an effective parent. Help me stay connected to you and my spouse through my devotional times, and help me balance my self-care with other-care, continually re-charging my batteries to stay up to the daunting task of raising my children up in the ways of the Lord, that in their old age they will not depart from them. Amen

Chapter Six

Hormones Will Wreck Havoc

Hormones are one of the sources of emotional intensity in the body. Along with the adrenal system and the neurotransmitters serotonin, dopamine, epinephrine, and norepinephrine, hormones set the stage for how we feel in any given situation. Typically, hormone-driven behavior is associated with females in general and adolescent females in particular. However, hormone-driven behavior and hormonal imbalance is functional across ages and stages and equally for both genders. As one of the sources of emotional intensity, hormones will wreak havoc in even the healthiest of families.

As part of the body's regulatory system, hormones are a good thing. The goal is not to dismiss or avoid them. The goal is to regulate them medically and behaviorally and to embrace them. One of the most elegant positive turn of a phrase I've heard is the description of the hot flashes in menopause as "power surges." Even the emotional and behavioral extremes of hormonal imbalance can add to the spice of life and the individuality of personality within your family. It's true that what doesn't kill you will make you stronger as a person and as a family.

In Mark's gospel, he describes a healing that Jesus unintentionally gave to a woman who had an "issue of blood." Conventional wisdom assumes this phrase refers to a condition of low-grade hemorrhaging associated with heavy menstrual flow. In Mark 5: 25-34, he recounts:

"In the crowd was a woman who had been bleeding for twelve years… The woman had heard about Jesus, so she came up behind him in the crowd and barely touched the hem of his garment. She had said to herself, 'If I can just touch his clothes, I will be well.'…She did and she was…At that moment Jesus felt power go out from him. He asked, 'Who touched my clothes?'…Then she told him the whole story. Jesus said to the woman, 'You are now well because of your faith. May God give you peace. You are healed, and you will no longer be in pain.'"

Praise God. Through him all things are possible. Praise the courage of this woman. She didn't resign herself to her condition. She had gone to many physicians and, no doubt, faith healers as well. She had spent all that she had in search of a healing. Her simple act of reaching out in faith to only touch briefly the hem of Jesus' tunic gave her the healing and relief she had sought for twelve years.

As parents, you want to be aware of the potential for hormonal imbalance to affect the temperament and interaction among family members. The ebb and flow of emotional intensity in the family is not of itself indication of dysfunction. Such ebb and flow is normal. It even defines a level of intimacy in relationship. Expecting consistency all the time in family functioning is a setup for difficulty.

At the same time, you want to assure that all family members are appropriately informed about potential for medical problems that may impact family functioning. You want to encourage medical follow-up where applicable, and develop emotional-behavioral-psychological means of addressing difficulties.

The Bower family is awash in hormones. Lauren is pre-menopausal. Her menstruation has begun to be more irregular. Jim is wondering if this is what life is all about. Emily and Jason are typical teenagers, each full of their own adolescent angst. Gracie has not started having monthly periods yet, but is beginning to find her shape and ask questions. How do they handle their particular slice of life? As parents, how do you chart a course through these troubled waters?

Chaos Central Re-Visited

"Get out, you little brat," Emily screamed.

All little Gracie had wanted to do was use the bathroom. She hardly cracked the door and stepped onto the threshold before being greeted with a harsh epithet from her big sister.

"Can't I ever get just a little smattering of privacy?" she bellowed as Gracie closed the bathroom door.

Lauren had heard the commotion from downstairs, where she was reviewing upgrade options for her department at work. She leaned on the dining room table, amid her spread of papers, and sighed. "Now what?" she labored.

Gracie charged down the stairs in tears. Lauren rose to meet her baby girl at the bottom of the steps. "Mama, Emily's being mean.

"What happened, sweetheart?"

"I was in my room playing," Grace sniffed and wiped away a tear. "I had to pee, so I went to the bathroom. I didn't know Emily was in there," she protested.

"You were just thinking about using the bathroom and then going back to playing in your room?" Lauren looked into her daughter's tear-filled eyes and her heart sank for her.

"Yeah, and Emily didn't have to yell at me." Grace stomped her foot to emphasize her conclusion.

"What Emily did hurt your feelings, huh." Lauren concluded as she drew her daughter to her.

"Yeah. Why does she have to be that way sometimes?" Grace paused before continuing, while her mom fell silent, giving Grace time to think. "Most times she's nice and I like having Emily as a big sister. But sometimes? Whew, she can be so mean. Why is that, Mama?"

Lauren paused to collect her thoughts and decide how much to share with Grace. She drew her away from the stairs and into the living room, where there was momentary peace and quiet. "Let me answer that question, Grace," she started, as they settled side by side on the couch." Grace looked eagerly at her. "You know, Grace, how your sister is a young woman, and you are still a girl?"

"She's just a know-it-all snot-rag, that's what she is."

"Grace, that's enough. We don't talk like that around here."

"Yes, ma'am."

Lauren shifted in her seat and then patted her daughter's hand reassuringly. "Well, being a young woman takes some preparation and some getting used to."

Grace cast a puzzled look toward her mom, as she waited expectantly.

"Well, part of the process is physical, not just being more mature."

"You mean, like, Emily's got boobies and I don't yet?"

Lauren chuckled, "Well, yes. That's one thing, but there's more."

"Like what?"

"Like, I think your sister is menstruating now." Lauren thought back to her daughter's request to borrow one of her tampons the other day. She smiled, thinking about how she had teased Emily that she could have the tampon, not borrow it. She didn't want that thing back after it had been used.

"Men stating what? You mean like talking like a man. That's why she yells at me for no reason?"

Lauren laughed and pulled her daughter to her in a bear hug. "No, sweetheart, not men-stating. I sure hope all men don't yell for no reason. I know your father doesn't."

Gracie looked puzzled. "The word is menstruating." Lauren articulated precisely. "It means losing a little blood through your vagina."

"Gross, oh yuck." Grace covered her mouth in mock horror. "What are you talking about?"

"You know how God told us to be fruitful and multiply? Well, the body has several things going on to let us follow God's will." Lauren paused to let this much sink in for Grace.

"Okay, so what's that have to do with men's...strut...a...ting?" Grace drew the new word out to practice saying it right.

"Well, near your tummy, right about…there," Lauren reached just below Gracie's belly button and tickled her. Her daughter released a peel of laughter. "is where a baby has room to grow inside you."

"Inside me? Is it there now? I'm not going to be a mommy, am I?" Gracie's voice raised in concern with each question.

"No, no, silly," Lauren assured her. "Babies happen in God's time and by his design. The Bible says that he knew you before you were even born, when you were in my tummy." She patted her tummy for emphasis.

"God's pretty smart, isn't he, Mama?"

"He sure is, and that's why babies happen only in God's time and by his will."

"Is my room there now, Mama?"

"Yes, but it's very tiny because you're just a little girl still." Lauren paused and then added, "And it's not your room. It's called a womb."

"Womb?" Gracie crinkled her nose. "You're making that up."

Her mama laughed as she shook her head. "No, sweetheart. I'm not making that up. It's a womb. It's a girl part that we are all born with."

"But you said I had a place here," she pointed to below her bellybutton, "where there was a room for babies to grow in."

"Yes. It's called your womb."

Gracie pondered for a moment and concluded, "So then it's a womb room?" She giggled at her own joke.

"Sure, honey, a womb room," Lauren tapped the tip of Gracie's nose and they both giggled.

"But, Mama," Gracie added after settling back down, "What's this have to do with menstruating?"

"Well, honey, you know that babies have to eat, even when they are in their womb room. We can't give them food or juice, so they get their nourishment from their mama's body."

"How's that work?"

"You know that our blood carries nourishment and oxygen to all parts of our body's. So, when a baby is in its womb room, it gets its nourishment from the walls of the womb through a tube that becomes your belly button after you are born."

"Whoa. Are you teasing again?"

"No, honey, for real." Lauren answered her daughter's puzzled look with an analogy. "It's like having two computer terminals on the same server. The electrical current, through the wiring behind the computer, keeps both terminals on."

"Oh, now I get it." Grace fell silent for a moment, thinking about it all, and then questioned, "But what's that have to do with menstruation?"

"Well, if a computer isn't being used, we turn it off, right?"

"Of course."

"Okay. So, when a baby is not in the womb room, the body doesn't need to store that nourishment in the womb. When the computer, the womb, isn't being used, God turns it off. The stored food for the baby comes out the vagina as a menstrual flow."

"Okay, now you're grossing me out again."

"Sweetheart," Lauren pulled her daughter to her and bear hugged her, "It's just God's way of preparing us for having babies and feeding them until they are born. He gave your daddy and me you through this blessing, even if it is a gross-out."

Lauren continued, "And that's why Emily yelled at you. She needed some privacy because she was getting grossed out herself."

Grace raised her eyebrows. "Huh?"

"Gracie, your sister is menstruating, and she was, uh, taking care of it while in the bathroom."

"When will I menstruate?"

"In God's time, little one, in God's time."

Lauren went on to explain to Grace the changes in emotional intensity associated with menstruation, and why it's called getting her period, until her daughter's attention wandered and she realized she had had enough explanation for one day. More would follow another time.

Normalizing the Reality of Hormone Impact

Lauren and Gracie's chat presents an excellent picture of family processing and normalizing how hormones will wreak havoc. She began by comforting her daughter, focusing on her feelings and the process instead of immediately trying to rescue her or find solutions. Her tool for such comfort was active listening. She physically moved closer to her and they both were somewhat out of the way in the living room.

She answered Gracie's questions at a level and in language she could understand. She paced Gracie with the discussion, making sure she understood and maintained interest. They laughed together, made up a personal giggle phrase (womb room), and interwove teaching and serious developmental matters into the fabric of the conversation. She also grounded the new words and knowledge in God's will. She only went on as long as she was sure Gracie was interested.

Finally, Gracie wasn't punished for barging in on her sister because her behavior was accidental. Emily wasn't punished for her harsh outburst because she was understandably surprised. She did, however, later apologize to Gracie for yelling at her, and they had some girl time, which reinforced Lauren's talk with Grace.

In your family, you might get three words out before your child seems to lose interest. If they are confused, clarify. If they are distracted, they are telling you, "That's enough for now." Nonetheless, however much you get to share, the process is positive and productive. You also set the stage for further sharing at a later time. You are practicing being a benevolent despot and using your earned authority.

The Emotional Side of Hormones

With hormonal imbalance, emotional intensity ramps up. For up to a week prior to beginning menstruation, many women retain water, gain weight, are more irritable, and will become tearful up at the drop of a hat. These are symptoms of premenstrual syndrome (PMS). With regular monthly cycles, PMS can be anticipated and concessions made.

For adolescent boys, whose hormones are rampant as well, just in a different way, the hormonal imbalance takes the form of hyper-competitiveness, focusing on sporting activity and physical fitness, posing and posturing by both dress and with "trash talk." Most adolescent boys are also, by their hormone-driven nature, very sexually oriented. Confidential surveys of this population confirm that nearly 60% of 13 year old boys have experimented sexually (Moore & Rosenthal, 2006). That percentage does not reach 60% for girls until they are 15 years old. Even churched teens battle sexual urges. In biblical times, girls became eligible for marriage shortly after menarche in part for this very reason. The Jewish custom of bar mitzvah is held on a child's twelfth birthday, and he is deemed a "man" in part for this very reason.

In your healthy, Christ-centered home, you will feel like you are swimming upstream when you place sexual intimacy in the context of God's will for married couples. Hold fast to your convictions, but be realistic and remain open to discussion. There are many teachable moments around issues of sexuality and hormonal imbalance.

For women, menopause offers another flood of emotional intensity. The dwindling reservoir of progesterone and testosterone creates wide variation in sexual drive. Most emotions become exaggerated in their expression. Body temperature fluctuates drastically as menstrual systems begin shutting down permanently. Many men will claim that women become highly irrational during menopause.

For men, menopause becomes a journey into the desert. Yes, men are menopausal as well. It just takes a different form. Lower progesterone and testosterone levels in middle-aged men lead to wide fluctuations in their sexuality as well. The emotional intensity features a sense of anomie, or lostness, questions of worth and fulfillment, and a fear of stagnation. For men who are out of God's will, extramarital affairs are rampant, lost youth is sought by claiming the perfect "trophy wife," and abrupt job changes are not uncommon.

Anticipating these pitfalls to hormonal imbalance will dampen the emotional intensity and increase a commonality, a sense that we are all in this together and we will get through it. Understanding, working through, and communicating about hormonal imbalance is pivotal in all ages and stages of life and family.

Learning the Concept: Exercise 17, The Emotional Side of Hormones

Consider the physical and emotional process of girls becoming women and boys becoming men. Individually, as a couple, or as a family, list 5 physical and emotional changes that most girls and boys experience during early puberty, as they become women and men.

Girls to Women	Boys to Men
1	1
2	2
3	3
4	4
5	5

The Brain Connection

Doris Trauner, MD, professor of neurosciences and chief of pediatric neurology at the University of California, San Diego School of Medicine, notes that the human brain doesn't complete its development until a person reaches his or her mid-to-late 20s (WebMD the Magazine, May, 2011). The parts still growing through adolescence are the frontal lobe and the parietal cortex. These parts house the executive function of the brain, including thinking through such tasks as planning, paying attention, and reasoning.

So, our teens are moody and irritable in part because of hormonal flux. They are spacey and forgetful because of incomplete brain formation. Each presents challenge to us as parents of teens. Take into account the relative immaturity of your teen's brain, as you help them regulate their bursting hormones.

Navigating the Troubled Waters

These troubled waters of hormonal imbalance can be navigated. While you need to take into account the nuances of bodily function within ages and stages, you are not at the mercy of these nuances. Anticipation and a proactive approach to management of hormonal imbalance will minimize its impact. Three tools apply for navigating these troubled waters:

Diet and activity level
Confidante Relationship
Journaling

Diet and Activity Level

Maintaining healthy diet, nutrition, and activity levels make good common sense at all times. The combination of multiple advances in medical science and technology, as well as our nation's embrace of healthy lifestyles and fitness, has led to extended life expectancies and fewer medical complications (see **Appendix 6**).

For girls and women to minimize the emotional impact of their menstrual cycle in particular, you want to increase your activity levels for at least the week before you start menstruating. Walking, jogging, sports activities on an on-going basis are terrific, but especially for that week before you start your period. Additionally in that time frame, you want to maintain a hypoglycemic diet. That is, drastically limit your caffeine and sugar intake at least in that time frame.

These measures increase your metabolic rate, helping your body to process your menstrual period more efficiently. Additionally, the increased activity gives you opportunity to channel the increase in intense feelings, burning them off as you exercise. As a parent, this is when you want to stock up on healthy snacks of dried fruit or flavored rice cakes, rather than Twinkies and other pure confectionaries. This also is when you want to challenge your teenage daughter to a game of tennis, go for a family walk, or throw the Frisbee back and forth. This kind of hypoglycemic diet and increased physical activity combats the impact of premenstrual syndrome on girls and women.

Learning the Concept: Exercise 18, Diet and Activity

Appendix 6 presents a weight management program that balances calorie counting and exercise. Many teens struggle with losing the "baby fat" of their childhood. Obesity in young people is at an all-time high. If you or your child or youth is overweight, review Appendix 6 and consider implementing this weight management plan. Weighing more than 20% above average weight for height and build is considered obese. In general, a healthy lifestyle that allows for 7-9 hours of sleep per night, is short on sugary snacks and long on exercise and physical activity benefits all of us. Such a lifestyle especially helps teens navigate the troubled, hormone-laden waters of adolescence.

Many teens are loathe to work out in a gym or jog through the neighborhood. However, recreational and scholastic sports provide excellent, supervised, physical conditioning. Such activities are available to children as young as 4 years old and on through high school. Beginner teams are available for just about any sport at any age through your local recreation department.

As a couple and as a family, talk about the sport activities each of you might like to explore and how you are going to do that. At first, brainstorm without consideration for time or expense. After you've exhausted your options, review the list with each family member and pare it down to the most realistic options. Talk about the details of participation, who does what, when, where, and how, to assure follow through.

Confidante Relationship

It's not surprising to me that God orchestrated the development of best friend relationships between our ages of 8 and 18. The latency, pre-adolescent, and adolescent ages are precisely when we need a best friend. This is not just someone with whom to hang out. They are not just a playmate or even a first love. Rather, the nature of best friend embraces the role of confidante. You can tell your best friend anything and they will not be shocked, or surprised, nor will they share a word of your stuff with anyone else.

The ages 8 through 18 also comprise the times of rapid emotional development and increasing of emotional intensity. Not only is your body changing with onset of puberty, but also your mind and emotions are changing. You gain the ability to think abstractly around age 12. Your abstract thinking enables you to label a wider array of feelings and intensity of feelings than the meager "mad, glad, sad, and bad" feelings of childhood.

Developing a confidante relationship offers you an outlet for these new and more intense experiences. Teenage girls will sequester themselves in one of their rooms for hours, and boys will make forts or tree houses, not because they want to shut out family, but because they are developing that confidante relationship. While you make a habit of checking on them periodically, by bringing them a snack or asking some innocuous question to be sure that nothing is amiss, it's nonetheless important for our children to have best friends outside the family. It is practice for the more mature emotional intimacy of adulthood and marriage.

Of course, parents have best friend, confidante relationships as well. When I hear one spouse describe the other as "my best friend," I know it is meant as an ultimate compliment. However, I also fear a certain enmeshment in the relationship that does not allow for best friend-ness outside of the marriage. Within trusting and moral boundaries, the concept of "boys night out" and "girls night out" helps couples and allows for emotionally intimate friendships that can complement healthy marriages.

Healthy marriages comprise roughly equal components of me, you, and us. The best friend is in the "me" category for each spouse. As such, these confidantes become an empathetic sounding board, mutual cheerleader, and moral compass for each other.

Some churches offer mentoring and accountability ministries for individuals and for couples. Often an older, established couple in a church will pair with newlyweds or a young couple/family as mentors. They meet occasionally to talk about how the marriage and family is going. The younger couple benefits from the wisdom and experience of the older couple.

Where there is a specific need or circumstance, some churches offer an accountability partner. This person is someone who has "been there, done that," and who can shepherd the partner through similar experiences. More generically, churches incorporate "prayer partners" into their intercessory prayer ministry. It can be comforting to know that, at a certain time each day, at least one other person in your church community is praying specifically for the very concerns that are on your heart.

I know of at least one church that hands out pagers to selected congregants in specific need. At various times throughout the day, when the pager goes off, the person in need knows that someone in the church has just prayed for them and their need.

The ultimate confidante relationship is one developed with your or your child's counselor. Individual, couple, or family therapy can fill an immediate, intense, time-limited need for people. In shepherding your children through hard times, I encourage parents to consider the six week rule. That is, most people have moods, emotional or behavioral fluctuations, or hard times that come and go. If the variance in your child's behavior is resolved within six weeks, it's likely a mood or stage developmental phenomenon. If it lasts longer than six weeks, it might be a symptom.

Symptoms are best addressed through the structure and consistency of counseling or therapy. While maintaining the client's confidentiality, a good counselor will develop a collaborative relationship between himself, the client, and the client's parents. A good marriage therapist will define the marriage as the patient and will develop a collaborative relationship with the couple in seeking the health of the patient.

At any level, whether structured or casual, the confidante helps individuals, couples, and families navigate the troubled waters fomented by hormonal imbalance. Having time and opportunity to share emotional intimacies with your confidante is another way to limit the havoc wrecked by hormones.

Learning the Concept: Exercise 19, Confidante Relationships

Research in social psychology indicates that most people have one or two best friends, a circle or crew of 6 to 10 close friends, and the rest of our relationships are family, co-workers, or casual acquaintances. Best friends usually fill the role of confidante.

In the space below, write the name(s) of someone outside of your family in whom you could confide your most intense and personal thoughts, feelings, and experiences. Is the confidante relationship reciprocal? Do you keep secrets well?

Journaling

At its best, journaling is a means of becoming your own confidante. It is a tool that can be used across the lifespan, beneficial to all ages and stages. Teenage girls are notorious for writing about "that cute boy three rows behind me in math class. I thought I would just die when I dropped my pencil and he picked it up and said 'here, you dropped this,' and then gave it back to me." This kind of journaling, a personal diary, is event driven, often inconsistent, and can be a good expression of innermost thoughts and feelings.

Therapeutic journaling, however, is more consistent, purposeful, and growth driven (see **Appendix 7**). It becomes an interactive tool, a means of relating to yourself at a deeper level and for purposes of positive change. When I prescribe such journaling in my clinical practice, I encourage certain structure.

First, dedicate time and space to the journaling process on a daily basis. Some people open a password file on their computer. Others hand write on a steno pad, the old fashion way. Second, the journal entries need to be relatively brief, no longer than a page. The reason for this is to avoid tangents and a time-consuming epistle. Your goal is to capture the main events of the day and your feelings about those events. Third, rank your journal entry on a scale of 1-10. While this number is arbitrary and subjective, over time you begin to calibrate your days and become a keener observer of your thoughts and feelings on the day. Depending on your focus, the scale could measure bad day to good day, more depressed to less depressed, more anxious to less anxious, more stressed to less stressed.

Therapeutic journaling is beneficial for several reasons. First, when journaling as a part of the bedtime routine, you release your mind from holding onto these thoughts and often sleep better. The thoughts become words on the page for you to reference whenever you choose. You don't spend sleepless energy trying to keep from forgetting them.

Second, you fine tune your observations to notice subtle, but important changes from day to day. As such, it is easier to pick up on positive steps toward your goal (less depressed, anxious, worried, or stressed).

Third, therapeutic journaling gives you opportunity to literally close the book on today, so that difficulties have less likelihood of bleeding over from one day to the next. Journaling is a safeguard against feeling overwhelmed because one day stops seeming just like the next.

Finally, by ranking your days on a scale of 1-10, you have a quick reference for adjusting your approach to the next day. If you have gotten an 8 some time ago, but are moving along mostly in the 4-6 range, then you have a positive reference if you have a bad day that ranks out as a 2. Flip through the pages to find the 8 and figure out what was so great about that day. Apply what you discover to your next day in order to bring your 2 up to a higher ranking. In this manner, you learn that you can control your days, rather than your days controlling you.

This kind of therapeutic journaling is most effective in monitoring and changing the moods of hormonal imbalance when it is a daily activity. After six to eight weeks of journaling daily, you will have developed the habit and the data to maintain positive changes in your life.

Learning the Concept: Exercise 20, Personal Journaling

Appendix 7 provides a detailed rationale and format for effectively journaling your thoughts and feelings. Many children and teens have had a diary, some complete with lock and key. Most diaries contain what I call "thematic journaling." Children are just getting used to writing down their thoughts and feelings. Entries may be dated, but they are mostly occasional and inconsistent. Children and teens frequently write descriptions of other people, romantic fantasies, and other such themes that help them define the relationships between them and the outside world. The high tech version of thematic journaling can be found on any My Space, Facebook, Blog, or Twitter account on-line.

Therapeutic journaling is another form of personal journaling. Your journal becomes a place for you to work out your thoughts and feelings, tackle personal issues, and commit to making positive changes in your life. It is most effective when journaling occurs daily.

Review **Appendix 7** and decide whether therapeutic journaling is a tool you can use to help you stay on track with your life. Do you want to use this vehicle for positive change?

SUMMARY

Everybody has hormones. Hormones are part of the body's early warning system and regulatory system. They affect your behavior, emotional intensity, and family relationships. Hormones will wreak havoc. They impact all ages and stages in a family.

Avoiding hormonal imbalance is not an option. Having hormones is a good thing. In healthy, Christ-centered families, the goal is to acknowledge, allow, and account for hormonal imbalance. Just as Jesus healed the woman with "an issue of blood for twelve years," we too can seek family healing from hormonal imbalance.

As parents, you want to monitor and guide your children's dietary and nutritional issues. Specifically in allowing for the female menstrual cycle, a hypoglycemic diet of low caffeine and low sugar content matched with increased physical activity will curtail the adverse impact of premenstrual syndrome.

Encouraging and utilizing a confidante relationship outside of the family will help you and your children ease emotional intensity. More structured confidante relationships include mentoring, accountability partnering, and keeping a prayer partner. By invoking the six-week rule, you will know whether a mood or difficulty might be morphing into a symptom. Where behavior becomes symptomatic, prayerfully consider counseling or therapy, an ultimate confidante relationship.

Finally, therapeutic journaling offers daily release of pent-up thoughts and feelings. It gives you an opportunity to be your own confidante when the other person is not available to you. It is a means of monitoring your days, noticing patterns, relieving a sense of being overwhelmed, and planning for more positive days tomorrow. Hormones will wreak havoc, but their impact can be accounted for and minimized by acknowledging them and taking specific steps to ease the emotional intensity.

Lord, we are all wonderfully and fearfully made in your image. You constructed our bodies in minute detail for specific, regenerative reasons. You gave us brains that far surpass the most elaborate and efficient supercomputers known to man. You gave us bodies that regulate, repair, relieve, and renew us daily. I acknowledge and accept that my hormones, and those of each of us in my family, will wreak havoc both individually and with potential fallout for the family. Help me to recognize the process, and find ways to minimize the emotional intensity within me and for my family. Amen

Chapter Seven

Teenagers Will Rebel

I t's not speculation; not a maybe. It's a fact and a certainty. Teenagers will rebel. As Christ-centered parents, we are charged with acknowledging the growth that rebellion brings, helping our teens minimize the adverse impact of their rebellion, and shepherding them into adulthood. These are no small tasks. Thankfully, "That which is impossible with man is possible with God." (Luke 18:27) Through God's grace and our hard work, our teens will rebel, survive, and successfully launch into adulthood.

Many years ago, a patient came to me for treatment for depression. She was 28 at the time. She felt lost, alone, in an autopilot marriage, and she saw no way out. On reviewing her history with her, I found out that her father died when she was 12 years old and that her mother never remarried. She became the perfect, dutiful daughter. She did everything to make her mother proud of her. She slipped into a role reversal with her mother, where mom became more inept and my patient became more caregiving to her.

After a few sessions of therapy with her, I hit upon a perspective that became life changing for her. She had never gone through any sort of adolescent rebellion. Her life circumstances at age 28 were, in essence, her delayed teenage angst. She wanted her life back, her own life. With this epiphany, my patient set a healthy course and completed therapy in short order with perspective and purpose.

In Scripture, several life-changing, indeed history-changing, teenage rebellions are chronicled. Remember, in biblical times, men and women became adults in their early teens. These were times where adult responsibilities and decisions were thrust upon struggling adolescents well before their bodies and emotions had caught up with them. Typically, teenagers rebelled against parental authority and, ultimately against God's authority.

For example, after Eve offered the apple to Adam (Genesis 3: 1-20 selected), Scripture notes, "The Lord God then asked the woman, 'What have you done?'" And, so, our sinfulness and rebellion from God began.

Further, sibling rivalry is often borne out of teenage rebellion. In Genesis 27: 32-36, the account of Jacob's rebellion is found. As Isaac lay dying, his eldest son, Esau, came to him after Jacob's deception.

"Who are you?" Isaac asked. "I am Esau, your first-born son." Isaac started trembling and said, "Then who brought me some wild meat right before you came in? I ate it and gave him a blessing that cannot be taken back." Esau cried loudly and begged, "Father, give me a blessing too!" Isaac answered, "You brother tricked me and stole your blessing." Esau replied, "My brother deserves the name Jacob, because he has already cheated me twice. The first time he cheated me out of my rights as the first-born son, and now he has cheated me out of my blessing."

Teens notoriously feel entitled to what is not theirs and to what they cannot afford. In Jacob's case, his two deceptions came at the expense of his brother, but put into play the house of Israel and God's plan for the Jewish nation.

Developmental Imperative

In the Jewish faith, bar mitzvahs and bat mitzvahs are celebrated on the child's twelfth birthday as a rite of passage into adulthood. The word "teenage" is a compound contraction that comes from the words "between" and "age." Literally, a teenager is between ages of childhood and adulthood. The Jewish rite of passage notes the point in time when the child becomes a man or woman. While this may be technically correct from a medical perspective of hormones and physiology, it misses the mark in describing the "sturm und drang" of the emotional side of adolescence.

Teenagers will rebel because such rebellion is the source of developing individual identity. The body is changing physically. The mind has begun to think abstractly. Rebellion sets the stage for the emotions to catch up with the mind and body. Without teenage rebellion, dutiful children become dependent adults. As parents, we are charged with providing our teenagers with the tools to become independent and responsible adults. While we don't promote teenage rebellion, healthy, Christ-centered parents will acknowledge their teen's rebellion as a good thing and will use it as a series of teachable moments on their teen's journey toward independence and responsibility. The result will be the successful formation of your teen's individual identity.

Conventional wisdom suggests that about 80% of our child's identity, temperament, and healthy choices come from life experiences before the age of five. In these formative years, we parents are the most available and consistent caregivers. We have control over 80% of what makes our children who they are. Subsequently, the relationships our children form in their early school years, roughly from age 5 to 12, account for about 15% of their identity. The remaining 5% of our children's identity comes from within, from their individual experiences through adolescence.

From this perspective, teenage rebellion is necessary, but really only a drop in the bucket of whom our children are as individuals. As parents, we draw on our faith in God, and faith in our previous parenting of our children in their formative years, to weather the storm and stress of teenage rebellion. However harsh or impactful this rebellion, when our children come from good stock, they weather the storms and grow from the stress.

Learning the Concept: Exercise 21, Telling Your Stories

Individually, as a couple, and as a family, write down 5 ways you rebelled (parents) when you were teens, 5 ways you see yourself rebelling (teens) now, and 5 ways you anticipate rebelling (children) when you become a teen. Remember, teenage rebellion is individual, personal, and purposeful. As you share your stories with your children and teens, you are not giving them permission to rebel in similar ways. Also, this discussion is an excellent opportunity for you to practice your Active Listening. Write down answers to the following questions.

In hindsight, why do you think you rebelled in the way that you did?

As children and teens, what do you think are some of the most harmful forms of rebellion?

Which ones seem to have the most dire consequences?

Revisiting Natural Consequences

As children test the limits of their environment, dependency-based and guidance-based parents set healthy boundaries and clearly define the rewards and the consequences for their children. When children become teens, parents also move from the parenting stage of guidance-based parenting to being the parent advisor. This developmental jump for parents acknowledges that your children are teens now and you need to partner with them, providing them sound advice, rather than just telling them what to do. The consequences that follow their choices are natural.

For example, Lauren and Jim Bower rarely got calls from school about their son Jason. Basically, he was a good kid, although he had his moments. During back-to-school night, the Bowers dutifully made the rounds with his teachers. They also made themselves known to the assistant principal, who was in charge of student discipline.

These preventive steps paid off the day Jason decided to skip school with one of his buddies. Oh, the misstep was innocent enough at first. Their bus had been late and Joey had suggested to Jason that they wait inside his house. His parents had already left for work. The bus subsequently came and went, so the boys decided to make a day of it.

Thankfully, Jason had an attack of conscience at about ten o'clock that morning. He called Jim's office and asked his secretary to write him a tardy excuse and come get him to go to school. Of course, the secretary told Jim, who in turn called the assistant principal. Although the consequences fell outside of the normal sequence of events for school discipline, Jim asked the assistant principal to simply meet Jason at the door and advise him that his school day was still six hours long, whether he arrived at eight o'clock or ten o'clock in the morning. Thus, Jason had to stay two hours later in school that day, resulting in his missing football practice as well. Because Jason had not had previous offenses, the assistant principal was okay with this "tardy" being just between the two of them and not put on his record.

Had his secretary written the contrived tardy excuse, Jason's ploy would have been successful and gone without accountability. Had Jim just left the assistant principal to continue to think inside the box, Jason's dad would have lost a teachable moment with his son. Jason would have chalked up the experience as punishment for having gotten caught. Because of Jim's creative thinking, Jason learned that his choices have natural consequences for which he is accountable.

With responsibility and good choices come opportunity, in Jason's case, opportunity to make football practice that afternoon. Jim brought home his object lesson in a chat with Jason later that night after each had gotten home.

Two weeks later, Emily and one of her friends were driving to the mall after school. They were in a hurry. Two guys at school had shown interest and the four of them scheduled the time to hang out together. As Emily was driving, the car sputtered to a stop. She was able to pull the car over to the side of the road. She called her dad in a panic.

"Dad, ohmygosh, I'm so glad you answered."

"Hi Em. Sweetheart, slow down. What's the trouble?"

"Jill and I are on our way to the mall. The car just died. I'm on the side of the road. You've got to come and get us!"

"Gosh, honey. I'm sorry for your fix, but I have clients coming in for me to go over their portfolio with them in ten minutes. They live an hour from here. I can't just pick up and bail you out."

"Dad, what am I going to do? The guys are waiting on us. I can't get in touch with them. We're out of gas and on the side of the highway."

After getting details about their location, Jim offered, "Tell you what, Em. Just off the next exit is a gas station. They'll let you borrow a five gallon gas can and you can bring it back to your car to get you enough gas to get there to fill up."

"You mean walk there? Dad, that's, like, over two miles."

"I know, honey. What a great opportunity for some exercise. Put your blinkers on. Stay well off the road. You'll get there and back in no time."

"Yeah, right, Dad. But it's hot outside, and that's four miles round trip.

"I didn't say it was a great solution, just one that is doable. I'm sure you'll take care of it. Gotta go now. See you at home. Love ya."

After Emily hung up from her dad, she called her mom. Mom also was busy and, incredulously, offered the same solution her dad had pitched. Emily felt dejected. She and her friend had started walking to the gas station when she remembered the Triple A card in her wallet. Her folks had put her on the family plan. She called the roadside service company. A truck came in forty-five minutes with enough gas to get her to the station.

They missed their hook-up with the boys, as it was time to get home. After telling her folks of her misadventure and the unfortunate, natural consequences, Jim seized the teachable moment to ask Emily how she might avoid such a difficulty next time.

"I guess I need to keep a better watch on the gas gauge, huh?"

For teenagers, natural consequences are often the best teachers of life's lessons. As parents of teens, you want to be available to help your teen struggle with the choices, assess the relative merits of their options, and support them in the resolution. Finally, we offer hindsight after the fact to help our teen avoid similar pitfalls in the future.

Restrictions that Work

As a measure of discipline, corporal punishment tends to lose its effectiveness as a behavioral deterrent after about age ten. If ever used, spankings are helpful in steering children away from bad behavior when administered by the same gender parent. However, the use of corporal punishment needs to be phased out as a youngster moves toward his teenage years. When correction is required for egregious behavior, most parents of teens prefer using restriction (**see Appendix 8**).

Typically, parents use a style of restriction that is too general, lacks time limitations, and suggests a process of "going to jail." Teens either rebel from this type of restriction or endure it, but with no subsequent, long-term change of behavior. Some teens have even told me that they are "on lockdown," and refer to their parent as "the warden." Such restriction is simply self-defeating. It reinforces the parents' power at the expense of the relationship.

For my undergraduate research as a psychology major, I put together a simple study of the effect of time-out on children in a classroom for emotionally disturbed students. In this unpublished study, as the student acted out, he/she was randomly given either a five-minute timeout or a thirty-minute timeout in the isolation room. I measured the student's self-esteem, relationship with the teacher, and understanding of the teacher's reason for giving the timeout upon their return to the classroom.

The results indicated that students with the shorter timeout maintained their self-esteem, continued a good relationship with their teacher, and understood why they had been given the timeout in the first place. Students with the longer timeout demonstrated a drop in self-esteem (e.g., "I'm a bad person."). They saw the teacher as mean. They had no clue of the rationale for their timeout and concluded it was "just another punishment."

Judgment, Compassion, and Mercy

Some years ago, I heard a sermon where the pastor described the relationship between judgment, compassion, and mercy. He was describing God's relationship to the Israelites, His Chosen People, who seemed to always be screwing up, asking forgiveness, doing well for a while, and then screwing up again.

As I listened to the sermon, I transposed what I was hearing to the parent-child relationship and behavior management strategies. I subsequently encouraged parents to trade in their correctional prison model of restriction for this godly relational model.

In the correctional prison model, many parents declare, "You're grounded until your forty." Or, they will leave the restriction too abstract and too open-ended, "Your grounded until you can prove to me that you get it." Even something less obtuse can miss the mark. Many parents who are frustrated with their teen's grade production in school will say, "You can't drive until you bring home all B's on your next report card."

Although well-intentioned, this kind of restriction is a set-up for failure if the restriction creates more work for you. Who has to go to the grocery store now when you run out of milk? Also, when the time frame is excessive, just like my senior research project, your teen will lose sight of the lesson, give up on getting off restriction, or wait for you to slip up and allow him the privilege before his restriction is up.

On the other hand, a godly relational model of restriction is more specific, time relevant, and encourages the teen to actively comply, with the incentive of shortening the time on restriction. Restriction becomes a progression from judgment to compassion to mercy.

Grace's Restriction

After talking to each other about Grace's treatment of her friends, Lauren and Jim decided to have a talk with their daughter.

"Hi, Grace," her mom began. "Come on in the living room here and sit for a while with your father and me."

"Uh oh. Am I in trouble?"

"What makes you say that, sweetheart?" Jim gestured to have his daughter come sit by him. She sat down and he gave her a reassuring squeeze.

Grace gently pulled away and turned to face her dad.

"Because, Daddy, you guys never call any of us into the living room unless we are in trouble." She sighed dramatically. "Okay. What did I do?"

Lauren smiled at the wisdom of her eight year old. She began to explain.

"Grace, you're such a sweet and beautiful young lady. You are smart, engaging, and creative. You have lots of friends and do lots of things. Girl Scouts, gymnastics, and cheerleading are all on your plate each week, not to mention Sunday school and children's activities on Wednesday nights."

"Okaaay." Grace arched an eyebrow, wary of the 'but' she feared would follow. Her father didn't disappoint her anticipation. "It's just that, honey, your mom and I have seen you bossing your friends around more, not letting them get their turn, wanting always to have your way."

"That's not fair," Grace protested. "I don't do that. I love my friends and they love me. If we do what I suggest, it's because they want to." She stood and began to tear up.

Lauren gathered her daughter into her arms, comforted her, and eased her to her seat between her and her dad. "Gracie, your daddy's not being mean. We just want to let you know what we are seeing." Grace sniffled. Her mom continued, "We've asked your Girl Scout leader, gymnastics teacher, and the children's pastor. They all agreed with our observations to one extent or another."

"What? Everybody knows about this?" Grace exclaimed and teared up anew.

"Honey, we wanted to be sure of what we were noticing and wanted to know if it was just at home or elsewhere as well," explained her dad. "If you continue being bossy with your friends, they won't want so much to be your friends anymore."

Grace and her folks continued to talk for a while, after Grace had calmed down some. Her mom and dad encouraged her to watch how she was with her friends for a week, using that time to practice being nicer and less bossy. They told her they would touch base with her the next week.

In that next week, Grace got into a fuss with a girlfriend on the school bus. Her teacher also wrote them a note about how Grace had gotten into a tug-of-war with a boy in her class over the football. She also baited Jason and went off running and screaming through the house when he started chasing her. Mom and dad again brought her into the living room.

"So, how's it going with the little self-improvement project we asked you to do?" Jim began.

"What do you mean?"

Mom added, "Grace, you know, we asked you not to be so bossy this week."

"Oh, that." She flopped on the couch and put her feet up. "Okay."

"Okay?" Dad gently slid Grace's feet back down to the floor. "Can you tell me more?"

"You know, okay. As in, I'm not being bossy anymore." Lauren sighed, not believing her daughter was as clueless as she presented. Grace noticed her mom's response. "What?" Grace defended, "I'm not being bossy. Ask any of my friends."

"Well, sweetheart, we have." Jim took his daughter's hand gently.

Grace's parents took turns telling her what they had gotten from the bus driver, teacher, and Jason. They expressed disappointment that Grace didn't make the effort to check her bossiness when given the opportunity. Her mom continued, "Hon, your dad and I have been thinking of ways to help you conquer this problem. We think a restriction will help you remember each day to be nicer to people, stop the bossiness, and assure that your friends continue to be your friends."

"What? Restriction? No fair," Grace erupted. "I haven't done anything wrong."

Jim reached for his daughter's hand, but she pulled it away. He continued, "Grace, you have done something wrong. We are charged by God to raise you up in the ways of the Lord, so that you will not depart from them. God is not mean or bossy, and we all want to be just like Jesus wants us to be."

Grace rolled her eyes as her dad got preachier. She looked at her mom and knew that she was in agreement with her dad. Her slumped shoulders and glum look told her parents that Grace didn't like it, but she was coming around to what they had been telling her.

"So," Jim mustered as much cooperative energy as he could. "This is our judgment. In an effort to help you learn ways to be more sharing, less bossy, more cooperative, less out there, doing your own thing, we're going to restrict you to being with your friends from after school to dinner time only at our house and in our yard. You may not go to one of your girlfriends' homes, even if you are invited. You can go to Sunday school and church activities as they are scheduled, but not to gymnastics or cheerleading practice for the next two weeks."

"Two weeks? That's too long," Grace protested.

Her father continued, undeterred. "You may have friends over each day after school if you want. This will give us opportunity notice how your efforts are going and to give you hints and prompts along the way." Grace rolled her eyes. Her dad concluded, "This is our judgment."

"Grace continued to protest, "Two weeks is way too long. I can be nice tomorrow. Just give me a chance. We have a cheerleading contest weekend after next. Can we do this after the contest?"

"Grace, enough," Lauren looked sternly at her daughter. "This is our judgment on this matter. It's up to you if we can give you compassion and mercy."

"Yes, ma'am."

Grace and her folks talked about what being nicer meant, and contrasted it with being bossy. As the next five days progressed, they found occasion each day to complement their daughter on her efforts. Jason even tried to pay Grace back by verbally baiting her one evening. Grace laughed at him and did not take the bait. They checked with church staff and got nothing but glowing comments from them about how cooperative Grace had been. While cooking supper the next night, Lauren took a moment with her daughter.

"Gracie, your daddy and I are so proud of you," she gushed. "You are really getting the idea about being cooperative and a good friend to others. We are going to show you compassion." Grace's face brightened. Her mom continued, "Instead of two weeks now, your restriction will be over in ten days from our last talk."

Grace pondered the length of time. She realized the restriction would still go through the weekend. She challenged, "Can I please participate in the cheerleading contest on Saturday anyway?"

Lauren smiled and told her daughter, "Just keep up the good work." Saturday morning came. Jim woke his daughter up earlier than usual for a Saturday.

"Honey, time to get up," he nudged her gently. Grace rolled over and smiled at her daddy. "You don't want to miss the cheerleading contest."

Grace lulled for a moment as her daddy's caution sank in. She bolted up in the bed. "You mean it?"

"No, I mean you did it. You've done so well with your restriction, making it a learning experience and reaching your goals, that your mother and I want to give you mercy. Your restriction is over."

"Yaaay." Grace hugged her daddy.

"Because your restriction is over, I guess you better get ready to let me take you to the cheerleading contest."

"Double yaaay" She hugged her daddy again, even tighter this time.

Why Grace's Restriction Worked

Jim and Lauren saw a behavior in their daughter that they did not like. Rather than identify and punish, they called her aside to make their observations to Grace. She wasn't in trouble. They hoped that bringing their observations to Grace would be sufficient for her to make the necessary changes. They also did not rely solely on their own observations. Rather, they made targeted inquiries of others who could add their observations.

Such expanded observations keep the exchange from being perceived as personal. Grace's parents also approached the problem behavior collaboratively. Grace was not the problem, but her behavior was problematic. Predictably, Grace tried to deny, minimize, and redirect, all in her effort to not take responsibility for her behavior. She also tested the limits, got teary, and even got a little mouthy.

By continuing to use active listening, Jim and Lauren were able to address their daughter's resistance without personalizing it or damaging her self-esteem. Their confrontation, followed by active listening, led Grace to ultimately accept their observations. Even then, her parents hoped that bringing Grace's attention to their concerns would cause her to change her behavior. They gave her a week to work on the changes independently. Research has shown that monitoring a behavior in and of itself tends to change the behavior in the desired direction.

When the change did not occur in that time frame, Jim and Lauren imposed a restriction. As parents, you want to actually use the terms—Judgment, Compassion, and Mercy. As this godly relational restriction becomes the norm, children feel empowered to embrace the learning opportunity, with the payoff of minimizing the length of restriction.

Finally, as all children, Grace tried to wear her parents down, divide and conquer, and avoid the accountability. Because Jim and Lauren were of one accord and remained consistent in the time frame, and because they each gave Grace positive feedback as the restriction progressed, Grace felt empowered and accountable, leading to the positive change in her behavior.

Learning the Concept: Exercise 22, Restrictions that Work

Appendix 8 provides a rationale and format for implementing the relational model for restrictions, which allows for a measured step-down from Judgment to Compassion to Mercy. Review this appendix and share your thoughts and impressions with each other.

What's the outcome of a correctional model for restrictions?
What's the outcome of a relational model for restrictions?

How does each model effect positive change in your child/teen's behavior?
Correctional Model
Relational Model

How does each model impact your child/teen's self-esteem?
Correctional Model
Relational Model

How does each model impact your relationship with your child/teen?
Correctional Model
Relational Model

Catch Them Being Good

Given that teenagers will rebel, as parents we can't catch them being good enough. Every time your child does something right, obeys, shares, listens, organizes, sets up his/her own accountability system, makes good lifestyle decisions, or follows through with the edict, What Would Jesus Do,? by all means, praise and reinforce their good choices.

If our children are comprised of 100 parts, what you pay attention to grows. If your child has 81 good parts and 19 bad parts, don't continually badger him about his bad parts. Doing so only encourages those 19 bad parts to become 22, 28, and more. If you pay attention to the 81 good parts, marking individual behaviors out with praise and attention, then those 81 parts become 85, 87, and more.

We would like our children to be perfect, but only God is perfect. He doesn't call us to be perfect. He loves us in spite of our imperfections. Can we love our children any less? Positive reinforcement and attention, the concept of catching them being good, increases our children's self-esteem, our relational bonds, and sets the groundwork for steering them through their teenage rebellion to successful adulthood.

Learning the Concept: Exercise 23, Catch Them Being Good

Children and teens will consistently seek your attention. Unfortunately, negative attention is usually easier to get than is positive attention. It's usually swift, immediate, and impactful. Positive attention generates a reward, while negative attention generates a consequence.

Industrial psychology teaches consultants the "sandwich effect" in providing meaningful consultation. As parents, and therefore consultants to your children, when your child needs incidental correction, use the sandwich effect. That is, start with a comment or affirmation, related to the event, which is positive. Follow the positive with your constructive criticism. Follow your negative comment with a concluding positive affirmation and encouragement.

Read the following examples of the sandwich effect. Bracket and put a **P** over the parts of the comments which are **Positive**. Then put an **N** over the part of the comments which are **Negative**.

1. _____ Sweetheart, you are getting to be such a big boy, using your knife to cut your meat. But you know what? If you hold it this way (demonstrate) it will cut better. Give it a try. I know you'll get it soon.

2. _____ Aww, man! Son you are getting some serious studying in tonight. I just don't think it's a good idea to keep the iPod cranked up and dance around your room if you plan to ace that test tomorrow. Turn off the music for just another twenty minutes, and I will come in to quiz you on what you've studied. Gosh, some day you're gonna make me a rich man with your music, ya know?

3. _____ Wow! Teaching you to drive, hon, is a breeze. You've got almost all of the rules of the road down pat. We need to get some more drive time in so you can practice what you know. Before long you will be driving like a champ.

Now, think of three circumstances in your home and with your kids where you can use this sandwich effect to guide them.

1.

2.

3.

SUMMARY

Teenagers will rebel. Even in the most godly, Christ-centered homes, our teens will screw up in great or small ways. It's not just a given, it is a requirement, as our teens forge their personal identity. To the extent possible, we need to back off and let natural consequences to their bad choices prevail. Experience is the best teacher. Having these experiences make our teens more willing to listen to our counsel.

Where possible, after identifying problematic behavior, give your teens opportunity to fix the problem themselves. This is an empowering experience and the stuff from which personal identities are forged.

However, teens will always test the limits and are loathe to be accountable. When their personal efforts fall short of the mark, effective restriction is a helpful parental tool. The correctional model of restriction, as in society, often just makes better criminals. The godly relational model of restriction uses the progression from Judgment to Compassion to Mercy. This progression allows the restriction to hold teens accountable for their actions, becomes a series of teachable moments, and empowers teens to minimize their restriction by giving them means to shorten its length. Ample use of positive reinforcement, praise, and attention are staple parenting tools to help teens weather the storms of adolescence and successfully launch into adulthood as independent and responsible adults.

Lord, we know that strength and faith come to us through adversity. As parents, guiding our teens through their adolescent rebellion may be our hardest task of all. Thank you, Lord, for your confidence in us. You gave us these children to raise up in your ways. A godly foundation in the formative years helps us stem the tide of rebellion in the teen years. Speak through us in these times, Lord. Empower us to help us empower our teens to be responsible, accountable, and a positive role model for their peers. We can do all things through Christ. Amen

Chapter Eight

Problems Can Be Solved

Issues and drama are a part of the fabric of every family life. Making every effort to raise your children "in the ways of the Lord, so that when they grow old, they will not depart from them," does not make families immune to the slings and arrows of life. In fact, as Christians, Jesus reminded us that we will suffer for our faith. Living in Satan's back yard, called Earth, is a spiritual battleground. What resources do we have at our disposal when the issues and drama of family life generate problems for your children? Through God's grace and our hard work, these problems can be solved.

First Things First: Not Giving Problems the Opportunity to Flourish

Some guiding principles bear repeating. First, active listening when your child is having a problem is your go-to response. Being an active listener to him will help him identify the feelings that are problematic and will challenge him to find his own solutions, with your guidance. This always affirms his worth, responsibility, and accountability, which is part of your goal in launching him into adulthood.

Second, problems can generally be contained to the extent that you balance self-care with other-care and manage your own stress. Children are the emotional barometer of their parents' feelings and mood. That is, she knows what you are feeling even before you know what you are feeling. She may not be able to articulate it, but her behavior reflects your mood.

Remember the Plexiglas pyramid? Above the pyramid is God. As your relationship is secure and emotionally intimate with God, you have all the resources to handle life's difficulties. As you feel fulfilled and energized within yourself, you have all the resources to embrace and cherish your life with your spouse. As you and your spouse are loving and in synchrony with each other, you have all the resources to raise a healthy, thriving family. The blessings from each level pour down on the next level.

Other tools that we have identified maintain this flow of blessing down the pyramid of relationships. Personal devotional time energizes your relationship with God. Balancing self-care with other-care helps you manage daily stress. Couple devotional time and check-in "How was your day dear" time revive your marriage daily, as do such activities as the occasional "date night." Family meetings to coordinate schedules and maintain home functions help focus your children and develop responsibility and accountability. Balancing play with work with school with devotion helps your children become well-rounded and Godly.

These principles and tools all help keep problems in check and at a minimum. And yet, because of Satan's influence and our living "in the world," we are vulnerable to problems. As a means of commiserating with and affirming patients I see in my office, I frequently suggest that we Christians have a bulls-eye painted on our backs. When we suffer from problems, it's an affirmation that we are generals in God's army. Satan doesn't care about the foot soldiers. It's the generals that can make a difference with our faith, so Satan targets us with problems. In Scripture, Paul referred to the "thorn in my side," to indicate how Jesus tends to us in our infirmity (2Cor 12:7-10).

The Big Three Problems: Depression, Anxiety, and Addiction

Remember, by nature and because of life circumstances, children are moody. That is, children, and parents as well for that matter, have moods. We get stuff stuck on our minds. We say things to ourselves in the moment that are irrational and self-defeating. Moods happen. They come and they go. As a rule of thumb, if you or your child gets stuck and gets into self-defeating behavior that lasts six weeks or less, then it's a mood. If it lasts longer than six weeks, it may be a problem. Problems need extra attention.

When Depression Strikes

Depression is a stuck sad mood. You are in a funk. You wake up in a funk and you go to sleep in a funk. You know that you are in a sad mood, but you can't seem to get unstuck. For children and teens, a clue is one-word, or brief, responses to your questions. Remember, kids do not answer essay questions very well. When you get brief responses, peppered with "I don't know" and shoulder shrugs, switch to multiple choice questions. You know your child well enough to offer several life circumstances that might be on his mind.

Three Tools for Fighting Depression

Therapeutic Journaling. Appendix 7 is an excellent tool to help you get unstuck. Rather than target how good a day you had, target how depressed you feel. Your journal entries reflect the day's activities and your feelings about those activities, with your ranking at the end of the entry giving the day an overall rating on a scale of 1-10. When ranking depression, lower numbers indicate deeper depression. A ranking of 10, then reflects the overwhelming joy of meeting God in Glory. Of course, we only get one ten.

Because of the nature of this therapeutic journaling, we can actually see our moods improve and the depression lift as we track it. Research in behavior therapy has found that daily rating of any behavior on a defined scale moves that behavior in the desired direction. When you or your child is stuck in a sad mood for more than six to eight weeks, this therapeutic journaling is an excellent foundation for positive change.

Get Active! Activity is an antidote for depression. It is very hard to be depressed if you are moving and doing. The "blahs" are like an oppressive cloud settling down on your life. Activity fills your mind with other things and goes a long way toward lifting that cloud. If your activity includes physical exercise, then that's even better. A twenty-minute workout daily will raise your heart rate above 120 beats per minute. That is the threshold for the brain releasing endorphins into your system. These are natural, feel good hormones that will lift your mood.

When people are depressed, they are usually thinking, "This is how it is and this is how it will always be." The first step in defeating this irrational belief is to shorten your time frame. Make an effort to get up at about the same time every day and schedule things for the day. The "do list" needs to be short and concretely doable. Each activity needs to be successfully completed within a half hour. Allow for down time between activities. Schedule no more than 3-5 activities per day. Over time, you will be convincing yourself that this is not how it will always be, because you are getting things done!

Use the AS IF Principle. When people are depressed, they don't feel like doing anything. They mope, complain, lie around, and do as little as possible. For teens, this seems to be a lifestyle choice. For people who are depressed, they feel like they have no choice but to be this way.

Depression robs people of the activation process. The battery is dead and the brain is not jump starting. If you don't feel like doing anything, how can you ever get anything done? The "as if principle" is a euphemistic phrase that I've developed to help people jump start their brains. When you don't feel like doing something, and you know that something will be good for you to do, simply act as if you feel like doing it. Once you, ever so reluctantly, start doing that which you don't feel like doing, your mood will improve because activity is an antidote for depression.

Therapeutic journaling, activity, and using the "as if" principle, these are excellent tools for pulling out of a depressive slump. For children, you will want to be very involved in the process of helping them out. Therapeutic journaling can be presented as a pictograph for youngsters. Activities after school can be planned, with his input into what's fun and what's planned for him. Outside activity is always a plus, both because of the vitamin D we get from exposure to the sun's rays, and also because of the movement that releases endorphins. Riding bikes, playing hopscotch, jumping rope all have these therapeutic benefits and cost nothing. Loading up on electronic gaming can be a distraction, but is not activity that will help him overcome depression. The "as if" principle can be framed as a game of "let's pretend," or as a hypothetical, such as, "If you did feel like it, how would you carry that out?"

Don't Be Anxious

Anxiety is the great inhibitor. Our children want to go and do, but they are afraid. What if it's not fun? What if I'm not good at it? What if they won't play with me? What if I get hurt? There are innumerable "what ifs" out there that will inhibit our children from having fun, if we let them. Anxiety presents at least with a profound sense of "I don't want to," or, "I don't feel like it." The child shrinks from participation. Younger children will cling to your pant leg. Older children and teens will retreat into electronics, appearing "too busy" to go and do.

At the negative extreme, children and adults can become panicky. With panic comes, multiple physical symptoms occur, such as rapid heart rate, physical trembling, difficulty getting a deep breath, feeling totally out of control and fearing imminent death. Such extreme responses to situations require your immediate attention. Take your child out of the immediate area, where her triggers are. Hold both of her hands in front of you, so that you are facing each other, and encourage her to calm down. Mirror the deep breathing you are encouraging her to do. Much like the talking during use of the nurturing-holding procedure, observe and praise her as she regains control of her feelings. As she calms, help her to talk about what just happened, a sort of debriefing, so that you can explore ways for the next experience to be more positive.

Three Tools for Overcoming Anxiety

Whose Problem Is It? When your child or teen is overanxious about something, you can help him ease his anxiety. First, it is vital to determine whose problem is it. After a thorough active listening discussion, you will have a foundation for addressing the anxiety.

One way to ease anxiety and determine a starting point in addressing it is to decide whether the worry is constructive or destructive. Constructive worry is worry about things over which you have control. If your child is worried about her grade on that spelling test tomorrow, then she needs to study those words some more tonight. This would be constructive worry. She has control over it, so help her develop a plan to conquer it.

Destructive worry is worry about things over which you have no control. If your child is worried about thunderstorms, this is destructive worry. When her worry is destructive, help her give it up, and give it to the Lord. "Let's pray about that one, Honey. Do you want to start?"

Gracie's Dilemma

The day for baseball tryouts had arrived. Jim had dragged himself out of bed early Saturday morning to get Gracie ready for the tryout. He was flipping pancakes at the stove when his little girl sleepily wandered into the kitchen in her jammies, with teddy in hand.

"G'morning, Sunshine. Today's the big day. Are you excited? I know I am. My little girl is getting all grown up and playing baseball with the boys."

Gracie trudged closer to her dad and gave an exaggerated sigh, "My tummy hurts. I think I'm gonna throw up."

Jim stopped cooking and guided his daughter to the kitchen table. "Here, Baby, have a seat." He felt her forehead, which appeared cool to the touch. "You okay?"

"If I'm sick, maybe I will have to skip tryouts this year and try again next year."

"Well, Honey, that's a possibility. I don't want you throwing up on the coach's pants."

Grace snickered at the mental image. She caught herself and then soured her mood again. "Do I hafta go, Daddy?"

"Do you want to go?"

"Of course I want to go. It's baseball. I've been playing just with the girls long enough." Gracie grabbed her tummy with both hands for effect. "But I'm sick."

Jim wrapped Gracie up in a bear hug. "It's okay, Baby. It's tough being stuck between something you want to do and not feeling like you can do it, isn't it?

Gracie perked up slightly, lifting her head toward the pile of pancakes staying warm in the oven. "I am kind of hungry. Those pancakes smell delicious."

"I put blueberries in the batter, just like you like. Batter up?"

Gracie giggled at the double entendre that reminded her of the tryouts. She held her tummy again and offered, "Maybe I won't throw up if I just eat one pancake."

Her daddy returned to the stove and shoveled two piping pancakes onto Gracie's old <u>Dora the Explorer</u> plate. He put butter and syrup on the pancakes and slid them over to her.

"Daddy, this is kid's stuff. I haven't liked Dora stuff since I was five."

"Aww, my little baby's all grown up now. She's all of eight. Now she's a ballplayer." Jim paused and looked at his daughter digging into the breakfast. "Are you feeling a little better now?"

"Maybe," Gracie held a long pause and then sighed, "but do I still have to go to tryouts?"

"Don't you want to, Sweetheart?"

"Of course I want to, but…" her voice trailed off.

Jim waited patiently for Gracie to collect her thoughts.

"What if they tease me because I'm a girl? What if I'm not good enough to make the team? What if I goof up and can't do it right?

"Wow! Jim exclaimed, "That's a lot of what ifs." He took a breath and thought for a moment. "You know, we won't be able to answer all of these questions until next year if you pass on the tryouts today. I would hate for you to spend all that time without knowing."

"Yeah, me too," Gracie sighed dejectedly.

Jim looked at the kitchen clock on the stove. "You know what? We have about forty minutes before we have to leave for the ball field. What say you and me tackle these questions before we head out? Sorta clear your head a little, okay?"

"My tummy does feel a little better now that I've eaten. Maybe I was just hungry." Grace thought for a moment. "Okay."

Many dads would have taken personally their daughter's reluctance to go to the tryouts. Many dads would have tried to teach their daughter responsibility by reminding her that she had signed up for the tryouts and that he had already paid out the registration. These dads would have missed a teachable moment with their daughter without giving her an opportunity to understand her reluctance and without trying to help her solve her problem.

In helping your child relieve anxiety, take time to decide whose problem it is, what the problem is, and what are the contributing feelings to the problem?

Developing A Quieting Response. Through active listening, Jim was able to help Gracie figure out all of the "what ifs" that were getting in her way. Teaching her to alter and deepen her breathing when anxious, while challenging her "what ifs," is an effective calming technique for immediate relief of anxiety.

Appendix 9 outlines the development of a Quieting Response (which I call *Chillin' Out*). With children and teens, in specifically anxious situations, it is helpful to write out both the "what if...I wonder" cohort lists and the positive, relaxing image.

Learning the Concept: Exercise 24, What If's into I Wonders

Following is the list, developed by Gracie and her dad, of her top five anxieties about going to tryouts. For each listed "what if" write down a cohort "I wonder." Be sure to include your presuppositional phrase as a positive conclusion to your "I wonder" statements.

What if...?	**I wonder...**
1. What if they tease me about being a girl and trying out for the baseball team?	1. I wonder how well I will be able to ignore their teasing & have a good tryout?

2. What if I'm not good enough to 2.
make the team?

3. What if I goof up and can't do it 3.
right?

4. What if they don't like me? 4.

5. What if I don't know anybody 5.
trying out?

Developing a Plus One Response is an excellent place to go for specific fears and anxieties. Suppose Gracie had told her dad that she was afraid of getting hit by a fastball from the pitcher during tryouts. She is okay with going to tryouts and with all that is involved, except for stepping into the batter's box and facing that fastball from the pitcher.

The pioneering behavior theorist, Joseph Wolpe, long ago developed a treatment for specific anxieties and fears that is still used widely today. Hallmarks of his theory are the concepts of systematic desensitization and successive approximation.

In this Plus One model, I encourage parents and their children to set the scene for your child to do whatever part of the behavior where she is already comfortable, and then add one more step toward the goal. You can help your child come up with a list of behaviors that works up to the goal she wants to accomplish.

For Gracie, she and her dad could make a list that includes the following:

1. Going to the ball park.
2. Preparing to bat.
3. Stepping into the batter's box.
4. Have the pitcher throw balls outside, without your swinging at them.
5. Have the pitcher throw balls over the plate, without your swinging at them.
6. Have the pitcher throw balls anywhere around the plate, without your swinging at them.
7. Have the pitcher throw balls over the batter's box with your getting out of the way.

8. Have the pitcher announce which ball will be thrown over the batter's box, with your getting out of the way of it, while swinging at good balls thrown.

9. Having the pitcher throw regular batting practice for you.

Each item on such a list would be a **successive approximation** of the goal of taking batting practice without undo fear and anxiety. Whenever your child locks up with fear, stop the progression, go back one step, and help her calm down. This would be the time to coach her on using her quieting response. Such calming techniques would effect a **systematic desensitization** to the anxiety, allowing her to go plus one on the list, until the list is accomplished.

Who's Got the Control? Treating Addictions

When most of us think of addiction, we think of the pathetic drunk, lying in the gutter, clutching a bottle of whiskey. Or, we think of the druggie, lying on the floor of a condemned building downtown, with a needle jammed in his arm. Both of these people are addicts, and they each describe an extreme view of addiction.

In fact, addiction is simply any behavior that has a hold of you, rather than you having a hold of it. Beyond the obvious drugs and alcohol addictions, other identified addictions include addiction to cigarettes, food, sex, prescription pain medicine, gambling, computers, gaming, and other electronics. While your family may have escaped any drug or alcohol addiction, how are you doing with these "lesser known" addictions?

Infants are known to have food preferences. A baby's palate is still developing and may not enjoy a variety of foods. Baby foods come in quite a variety, however, to help babies expand their palate sensitivities. Many parents struggle with toddlers who will only eat certain foods. If you give in to his acceptance of only hot dogs and mac 'n cheese, are you doing your son any favors?

Some children experience "sensory motor integration" issues. They will only wear certain fabrics. They don't like their hair to be washed. Their socks have to be right side out when they put them on. They cringe at unexpected noises or commotions. If you accept that she is "just different," are you doing her any favors?

Some pre-teens and teens isolate in their rooms, gaming on their computers 24/7, or texting on their phones, or updating their Facebook status. Even with putting parental control programs on their electronics, if you rationalize that it's just a stage, or that he likes his space, are you doing him any favors?

If, when you examine your child's behavior, you conclude that the behavior has control of him, rather than his having control of the behavior, then you may be confronting an addiction.

Three Tools for Defeating Addiction

Identify, Confront, and Own It. Any addiction recovery has a Twelve Step flavor to it. First is to accept that the behavior has control over your child. If, after much observation and prayer, you and your spouse agree that this is the case, then you must confront him and make your case. To do less is to enable him in continuing his addiction.

Very few children and teens will respond with a helpful, "Gosh, Mom, you are so right. I'll fix that right away." So expect denial and rationalization. Use your active listening skills to settle down his feelings about being confronted, but then renew your concerns for his behavior.

While some addictions require abstinence to start recovery (alcohol, illegal drugs, cigarettes, and gambling), others are in the "too much" category, but are necessary for life (food, sex, pain medicine, electronics). Those in the "too much" category require negotiation with your child, with your goal being his owning responsibility for his behavior and agreeing to limit it to your wishes.

Start Early and Monitor. Being very concrete in their thinking, toddlers and children will typically respond to "the rules." You can stop many behaviors by simply saying, "I'm sorry, Sweetheart, but that's the rule." Of course, as children age, they come to challenge the fairness of the rule. The sooner rules are in place, about eating habits and electronics, for example, the easier these potential addictions can be handled as children get older.

One rule to help picky eaters is simply instituting "The No Thank You Helping." Offer your child new foods, or ones he has previously rejected. When he rejects the serving, tell him the rule is that he must eat at least a "no thank you" helping. If it is peas, for example, give him just three peas, but require him to eat them. Your serving will challenge his palate to grow, and he will be complying with your expectations.

For electronics, I've known parents who build electronics usage into their house rules or into a behavior management system, as a reward for reaching target behavior. Some computers have a timer app, so that the computer automatically shuts down after time is reached. Gaining extra time with electronics is paired with better grades, or an equivalent time with family, doing family activities, or completing chores. This becomes a win-win solution for your teen and for you.

Cold Turkey. This phrase is associated with stopping an addictive behavior on your own and by sheer willpower. Hardcore members of AA or NA think going off, and staying off, booze or drugs cold turkey is impossible. These addictions require group effort and accountability, working a twelve step program, getting to meetings, and working with a sponsor.

For children and teens dealing with food, cigarette, and electronics addictions, you will want to challenge them to go off cold turkey. It is a nice response to his denial of having any problem at all. Have him stop his addictive behavior for two months, thus proving to you that he is not addicted to that behavior. If he fails, you are more likely to break his denial. If he succeeds, supplementing more positive behaviors for the addictive ones in the process, then he will likely not go back to the intensity of his addictive behavior which came to your concern in the first place. Remember, two months is the minimum time for new habits to develop.

SUMMARY

Ages and stages, we all go through them. Moods, we all have them. As much as we work on the Christ-centered parenting of our children, we, and they, are still in the world, which is Satan's back yard. Christ calls us to be in the world but not of the world (John 17:15-18). So, we will have problems. And yet, through God's grace and our hard work, problems can be solved.

Depression, anxiety, and addictions are the major areas of mental health problems that we all encounter to a greater or lesser extent. The tools offered for each of these problem areas are preventative in nature. Working them into your parenting your children as Christ would have you do, will give your children opportunity to get a handle on these things before they get out of control. Active listening, when your child presents a problem, is always your go-to response.

If he seems depressed, encourage his therapeutic journaling. Structure his activities more, so that he has the benefit of Christian fellowship with friends and family, and so that he stays busy. When he wants to just hole up in his room and wish the world goes away, encourage him to use the "as if principle."

If she seems anxious or fearful, use your active listening to help her define the problem more clearly. Is it constructive worry or destructive worry? Help her focus on stuff over which she has control. Teach her to chill herself out by developing a quieting response and turning "what ifs" into "I wonders." For specific fears, help her use a Plus One approach to problem-solving.

If you fear that one or more of your child's behaviors might have control over him, help him stop addictive behavior by identifying, confronting, and owning it. Start early with discussion of "the rules," and monitor the frequency of behavior that concerns you. Challenge your child to go "cold turkey." This is a win-win situation. If he succeeds, problem solved. If he fails, he is more likely to embrace your ideas on getting a handle on his problem behavior.

Once you have identified a problem behavior, start using these tools. Give it six to eight weeks. If you find little or no success, then consult your child's pediatrician first. Counseling and/or medication may be in the mix if these tools have little impact.

Lord, embrace my efforts to be there for my children in mind, body, and spirit. Give me wisdom and discernment as problems arise. Help me to use effectively the tools I have learned. Help my children to see You through me, and guide me in steering them away from the ways of the world and toward your Light. We love you, Jesus. Amen.

Chapter Nine

The Principle of
Responsible Freedom

People throughout the ages have fought wars to obtain or retain their freedom. Living free is a fundamental right of all civilized societies. Jesus came to set the captives free (Luke 4:18). All that teens really want also is to be free. They will be creative and expansive in their efforts for freedom. Add the adjective "responsible" to the mix and teens efforts often fall short of the mark. Responsible freedom for our teens is the goal of Christ-centered parenting.

Freedom and attention have similar components. Each is a sought-for goal. Each has either positive or negative connotation. Each has absolute qualities. For attention, negative attention is easier to obtain than is positive attention. Typically your parental response to a tantrum is quicker and broader than is your response to your teen bringing home straight A's.

Similarly, freedom borne out of irresponsibility is perceived as easier by teens because there is no accountability component. How many times have you told your teen, "Well, son, if you had asked, I would have gladly given you permission. However, since you just left and I didn't know where you were or when you would be home, I have to ground you."

When teens are responsible in exercising their developing freedom, however, their rewards are longer term and character building. Parents who exercise the principle of responsible freedom with their teens in essence say to them, "I will give you as much freedom as you demonstrate responsibility for. The more responsible you are, the freer you are of my supervision and oversight. However, if you become irresponsible at any time, I will have to pull back on your freedom until you can demonstrate more responsibility."

Exercising the principle of responsible freedom with our teens provides a collaborative effort in the teen's developmental goal of forming a personal identity. The accountability of parental oversight and supervision helps the teen build trust and integrity. Finally, teens who exercise responsible freedom are much better at making healthy, positive choices for themselves.

Christ-Centered Parenting and Responsible Freedom

In Scripture, Jesus' parable of the dishonest manager speaks to elements of responsible freedom. In Luke 16: 1-13 (selected), the author records, "A rich man once had a manager to take care of his business. But he was told that his manager was wasting money. So the rich man called him in and said, 'What is this I hear about you? Tell me what you have done! You are no longer going to work for me.'...That's how it is! The people of this world look out for themselves better than the people who belong to the light...Anyone who can be trusted in little matters can also be trusted in important matters. But anyone who is dishonest in little matters will be dishonest in important matters. And if you can't be trusted with what belongs to someone else, who will give you something that will be your own?"

Just as the rich man in the parable provided for his manager and entrusted him with material resources with which to do his job, so too do we as Christ-centered parents provide for and entrust our teens. The car she drives; the roof over her head; most of the food in her belly and the clothes on her back come from our resources. We give these resources gladly to our kids because we love them and we are charged by God with their upbringing. Most teens, however, take these gifts for granted. Most teens feel entitled to a luxuriant appointment and lifestyle.

The manager made bad choices and a mockery of the rich man's largesse. When the rich man found out, he called his manager on the carpet. Here, Jesus demonstrates the parental principle of responsible freedom. As our teens make good choices and manage parental resources with consideration and accountability, we gladly support their lifestyle and growing freedom. When we feel ignored, taken advantage of, and discounted, we need to step in to our teen's growing freedom and reassert our authority.

Learning the Concept: Exercise 25, Responsible Freedom

What is it? Write down in your own words what this phrase means to you. How do you see the Principle of Responsible Freedom applying to your teen, or to your children as they become teens?

The Rules

When my daughter was a young child, she taught me a valuable lesson. She had been caught in a minor mistake and I punished her. As she sulked on the time-out bench, she told me, "Daddy, if I had known you were going to give me a time-out, I never would have done it." I learned then to be clear with the rules, and pre-determine both reward and consequence related to following the rules.

Jason's Rite of Passage

Lauren and her youngest daughter, Gracie, were finishing up Grace's homework at the kitchen table. As her mom began to prepare a salad for supper, Gracie puffed her chest and pronounced, "Jason's got a girlfriend. I saw them kissing as she dropped him off after school the other day."

Lauren blanched. "Excuse me, honey." She caught her breath. "Say that again?"

"Her name is Courtney. She's a tenth grader and has her license. She's kinda cute," Gracie concluded, "but I don't see what she sees in Jason."

"Older? She drives?" Lauren felt stunned and she tried to let the facts sink in.

"Yeah, there were bunches of kids in the car. I guess she thinks she's all that."

Her mom continued preparing supper and prayed silently for Jim to get home from work quickly. They had to talk.

As Lauren and Jim retired that night, they talked about Jason and his new girlfriend. Their son had had bursts of girl interest in middle school, but nothing lasting or serious. Going together amounted to talking on the phone and walking with each other between classes. They recalled, however, that they had to correct their son on one occasion when he had kissed his current girlfriend in the hall at school and they got caught for engaging in a restricted PDA (public display of affection).

"That was kid stuff back then," Jim concluded, "But, if Grace is right about the details, then I think we need to sit Jason down soon and sort this out."

Lauren agreed and added, "You had the 'sex talk' with Jason several years ago. I know he's aware of all of the parts and specifics."

"Yep, we covered all the bases," Jim chuckled lightly. "He surprised me with how much he already knew."

"Jim, you are so '70's," Lauren smiled and nuzzled her husband. She then added, "I think I want to give him the 'girl's point of view,' and find out more about Courtney, without being too intrusive."

Jim agreed and concluded, "Then we need to pull out the rules. Emily had no problem with the rules when we talked to her. Of course, she wasn't as interested in dating as Jason is." He paused to think. "Jason's going to be a challenge."

Later that week, after Lauren had given her son the 'girl's take on all of this,' she and Jim pulled Jason into the living room after his sisters were otherwise occupied.

"Okay, Son," Jim started, "your mom has filled me in on Courtney and how you two seem to be hitting it off nicely,"

Jason rolled his eyes as he nonchalantly responded, "Whatever."

"Jason, be nice," Lauren chided, "Your father and I need to be serious with you for a moment."

"Okay, I'm sorry," Jason relented. "It's just that none of us likes these talks in the living room, but we all get them at one time or another."

"So, I guess this is your turn," his dad concluded.

Lauren shifted toward her son and smiled. "We both just want you guys to get a good, productive start to the next stage." Jason shrugged. His mom continued, "And what has Emily told you about this specific talk?"

"What? Hey, how do you know about that?" Jason protested.

"Ve have our vays," Jim curled his lip in a mock sinister way. Lauren shoved him away playfully, and then turned her attention back to their son.

"When we asked you to meet us here after we got back from church," Lauren continued, "we figured you made a beeline to Emily to get some tips. She hasn't dated much because she dives so deeply into her studies,"

"A habit, I must say, I would love for you to pick up," Jim interjected.

Jason glanced at his dad momentarily and mouthed under his breath, "Yeah, like that's gonna happen."

"Okay, you two," Lauren returned to her thought. "As I started to say, even though Em doesn't date much, we still gave her the rules by which she could date if and when she wanted to. Soo," she turned to her husband.

Jim picked up Lauren's cue. He started to respond, but thought through it all again. "Now wait. I have another thought." He turned to his son, "Jason, what do you think the rules should be around this girl, dating, and the whole car thing?"

Jason stumbled momentarily, as he was caught off guard by his dad. He had expected Dad to launch off another diatribe that ended abruptly with, 'because I said so.' He regained his composure and rose to the challenge. "Well, let me see. I should be able to see Courtney any time I want, as long as my homework is done and my grades don't fall. I've got my learner's permit, so I think I can drive if she is in the car with me. And, uh, I need to check in with you from time to time?" Jason tongue-in-cheek added, "or whenever I need money."

Lauren and Jim exchanged glances, smiled, and each shook their head. Lauren asked, "Do you want to lead off, or should I?"

Jim responded, "Oh, I'll take this one."

Jason began feeling invisible and chimed in, "Hello? Still in the room."

Jim took a long breath. After asking Lauren if she minded keeping track of the rules by writing them down, he launched into the discussion with his son.

"Good effort, Son. I give you credit. You are right that your homework and grades come first." Jason smiled with self-satisfaction. "You are also right that we need for you to check in with us when you are on a date. However, there are some holes in your thinking, not to mention some legal violations."

Jason's grin faded. "What? Where? I think I'm good to go."

Jason and his folks sparred for a while. Lauren explained the relevant laws about driving with a learner's permit, who the legal driver in the car can be, curfew laws, car occupancy laws, and laws against clowning and cruising. Jim added clarification about the specifics of calling home to check in and how 'talk to her any time I want' probably was not going to fly.

After more discussion, parrying, and effort to employ active listening and productive clarification, Jim concluded, "Okay, so let's give your dating Courtney, or anybody, a fresh start, now that we are all on the same page." He smiled back and forth between his son and wife. "Speaking of page, Lauren, what have you listed?"

Lauren reviewed the list. "Your father and I would like you to invite Courtney to our family cookout next Saturday. We want to get to know her. Also, tell her that you'd like her to have her mom call me to chat. It's fine that Courtney's a little older than you, but the driving laws restrict who can ride with her until she has her license at least six months.

So, no single car dates, and no double dating, until both of you have passed the age of license restrictions for teenage drivers. She's welcome to come over here, or I hope you're welcome to go over to her house, any time up to 9 PM on school nights and 12 midnight on non-school nights. No closed bedroom doors at any time. When you two find a larger group fun time together, like church youth activities, clear it with both sets of parents and you are good to go.

Finally, for the time being, we need to know your itinerary and we need a call from you when you make changes about where you are and who you are with." Lauren then turned to her husband and added, "I guess, Jim, now is the time to let Jason have a cell phone, so that he can easily reach us as things happen."

Jason brightened with his mom's last comment, as he had been lobbying for a cell phone for six months.

Jim reached into his pocket and retrieved Jason's new cell phone. He gave it to him. "Here ya go, Son."

"Awesome." Jason's eyes lighted up as he turned the phone over in his hand and then turned it on.

Lauren turned to Jim and concluded, "Anything else we should add?"

"I think that's a start. Let's talk next Sunday after our cookout, and see how it goes," Jim responded. "Also, let's make copies of The Rules for each of us to have, just so we stay clear about everything."

Jason repeatedly admired his new phone, looking as though his brain had stopped taking in the discussion after he got the phone. Jim waved his hand back and forth in front of Jason's face, and Jason came back from laa-laa land.

"Now, Son," Jim started, "We want you to have this cell phone because your mother and I believe you are responsible enough to handle it and to use it wisely. However, it is a privilege and also leverage. We want you to be responsible with the freedom we have given you. We expect you to be trustworthy and accountable."

"Not much freedom with all the rules you guys put on me," he groused.

"Welcome to adulthood, Son," his mom piped in.

"The rules merely give us feedback to continue to feel comfortable that you can handle increased freedom, as you are now becoming a young adult," his dad clarified.

His folks concluded the meeting with their son by reiterating how the principle of responsible freedom works. Jason did not like The Talk, but accepted it reluctantly. He felt encouraged when his folks added that his following the rules would be the pathway to his having more freedom and eventual launching into full adulthood.

Collaborative Effort and Developmental Stages

The Talk is the pivotal point around which parents and teens explore newfound freedoms and stage development. At around age 12, young teens begin to explore issues of personal identity. Both Erikson (1959) and Gesell (in Ilg, Bates, & Baker, 1992) refer to turbulent times in the early teens because of the influx of new hormones that fire off new exploratory and expansive behavior. In the years from ages 12 to 15, teens may seem like alien species and parents may tongue-in-cheek ask, "Who are you and what have you done with my kid." The Talk helps keep teens in check and on the same page with their parents in the growing and learning process. For teens, Erikson's stage of identity formation is a process that, in today's culture, may take them 10 to 15 years to complete. Some current researchers extend the stage of adolescence up to age 30, subdividing it into early adolescence (ages 12-18) and odyssey (ages 19-30).

Parents also are evolving in this time frame. As children move into adolescence, parents move from directed parenting to advising. As adolescents become adults, parents move from advising to consulting. These parental stage developments reflect your child's mastery of responsible freedom.

Both teenage and parental stage development is never smooth and problem-free. The Talk, a subset of family meetings, helps both parents and teens stay grounded in the reality of the current circumstances. Parents measure out wisdom and increase teen responsibilities as teens are open to accepting them. As teens rebel, freedoms are more restrictive. When teens are responsive to consequence and teachable moments, working their way through the process of Judgment, Compassion, and Mercy, their growth into eventual responsible adults lurches forward.

Parents and teens stay connected in a substantive way to the extent that Talks and check-ins become regular and normal. With your use of active listening and understanding, your teen will come to value these times together and appreciate the collaboration of measured oversight and supervision as part of the growing process.

Learning the Concept: Exercise 26, The Rules

As a couple, and then in family meeting, discuss the Rules of your home and family. Be fairly specific. While "Do unto others as you would have them do unto you" is universal, think in terms of, use your inside voice when inside, and, walk—don't run in the house. Rules can refer to values, collective good, or morals, as well as personal safety, healthy relationship, or good habits.

In the space below, write down the top 10 rules governing your home, family, and lives. Remember to use your active listening. Draw out the discussion as to why certain rules should be included on the list. Brainstorm, but as parents, you retain final word on what's included on the list.

1.
2.
3.
4.
5.
6.
7.
8.
9.
10

Accountability and Oversight Build Trust and Integrity

Accountability and oversight, or supervision, are the backbone of every growth project. Personal growth, corporate growth, and growing up young adults all require elements of accountability and oversight. Accountability can be individual or interactive. If I wanted to lose significant weight, I might consult a nutritionist and/or personal fitness trainer (interactive) who might set goals for me and provide counsel on reaching those goals. I might also graph my weight loss and body mass index (individual) to help me stay on track and provide incentive for reaching my goals.

Oversight, by definition, is always interactive. Teens talk about "the Man," which usually refers to police or other authority figures who are out there to watch and to help them stay on track. Thankfully, we have a loving, involved God, "the Man upstairs," who guides us in making good choices. Children and teens who grow themselves up, by virtue of absent, self-absorbed, or otherwise uninvolved parents, are rudderless. Lack of oversight results in lack of direction. The positive interaction between you, a Christ-centered parent, and your teen gives your teen direction, encouragement, and hope that he can make that harsh journey from childhood to adulthood.

With accountability and oversight, teens develop good character, specifically the qualities of being trustworthy and having integrity. As teens function with integrity, in essence, "I mean what I say. You can count on my words to be honest," then they build self-confidence. As teens demonstrate trustworthiness to you, in essence, "I will do what I say I will do and if things change, I will tell you," then they begin to trust themselves more and they exercise good judgment. The trust and integrity that comes from parental accountability and oversight are the building blocks of every teen's personal identity, which is the developmental goal of adolescence.

Roy Benaroch, MD, the WebMD Children's Health Expert (WebMD the Magazine, 2011) encourages parents to promote accountability and oversight with their teens by setting limits, modeling appropriate behavior, and teaching them cause and effect.

Learning the Concept: Exercise 27, Accountability and Oversight

These two functions are your part of the collaborative effort to raise your children in the ways of the Lord. For teens, an example of accountability is having them call you when their plans change while they are out. An example of oversight is having your son invite his new girlfriend over for a family dinner and the evening as a means of everybody getting to know each other.

In the space below, write down 5 examples of requiring accountability and 5 examples of providing oversight for your teen.

Accountability
1.
2.
3.
4.
5.

Oversight
1.
2.

3.

4.

5.

The Pathway to Adulthood

As teens make healthy, positive choices, they are forging a pathway to adulthood. As Christ-centered parents, we help our young adults stay the course. Exercising the principle of responsible freedom in parenting teens provides them with valuable mid-course corrections.

Consider the space exploration program by analogy. Every space launch has main thruster engines and many thousands of pounds of fuel to break free from the launch pad and escape the earth's gravitational pull. It would be a lot safer, of course, to simply stay on Earth in our warm, comfortable environment. However, we are explorers by nature, and so we launch into space.

After we are free from Earth's gravitational pull, the main thruster engines are cut loose. No turning back now. We then deploy booster rockets to maintain orbit and, in essence, stay the course. If we have a target, such as the moon or catching up with and docking at the space station, then we employ multiple small rockets positioned strategically on all sides of the launch. These rockets are used to fine tune our trajectory, so that we eventually hit the target.

We rely on an extensive ground crew to help with the launch and journey, but the captain and crew of the space vehicle do the manual labor and make critical decisions on the way. Without the full complement of planners, designers, technicians, and ground crew, however, the captain would have much less chance of success in space exploration.

Such a journey is similar to parenting. The launch is the birth of our children. The mother's labor and literal push is the thrust of the launch engines. The booster engines and the multiple small rockets surrounding the spacecraft are the direction, advice, and counsel we provide our children and teens on their journeys. When teens invariably veer off course, the principle of responsible freedom provides just the right nudge to help them get back on course toward their target of independent, responsible adulthood.

From Advice to Counsel—Mission Accomplished

As our teens exercise responsible freedom, we can bask in the sunshine of parenting success. Your advice during the turbulent teens can become needed counsel for your accomplished young adult. You become the expert consultant.

Expert consultants in business have three distinct qualities. First, they know their subject matter thoroughly. What they don't know, they find out. Second, they are invited into the company because of their expertise. They are given opportunity to collect needed assessment data about the subject of their consultation. They do so within an agreed upon time frame, and then they formulate a presentation. Third, they make the presentation to the business party with whom they contracted, answer questions, make recommendations, and most importantly, they then leave. Whether or not their recommendations are implemented is irrelevant and none of their concern as a contractor.

As expert consultant to your young adult children, your role as consulting parent follows these exact guidelines. By virtue of age, proximity, and experience, you are an expert to your children. To the extent that you have travailed successfully the developmental stages of parenting, and to the extent that you have emotionally bonded with your teens, they will seek out your counsel.

Now that they are launched, the parenting principle of responsible freedom is managed not by you, but by your offspring's common sense and by the laws of God and of the land. You are free to counsel however you choose. Your offspring are free to take your counsel or leave it. However, because you are important to your teens and they know and respect what you have to offer, they will come to you for wise counsel.

Your son or daughter is not sure where to go to college. There are so many factors to consider. Or, they are entering the work force and don't know how to go about it. Or, they are moving out but need roommates to make rent more reasonable. What makes a good roommate? Or, they are moving far away to "seek their fortune." How do they navigate foreign waters? While they will muddle along, ask friends, consider attaching to an older peer, and seek other counsel, you are their parent. They will seek you out. Let them.

Parents who force their opinions or will on a child of any age risk backfire. You may have the best counsel, but if your teens do not ask for it, you run the risk of rejection. And justifiably so. You have spent all those years supporting their developmental growth through the stage of identity formation and autonomy. Imposing your opinion or will on them goes against all that good work you have previously done to "grow your child up in the ways of the Lord."

Because you are around your teen during their deliberations about life-changing events, you may become impatient to be asked for advice. In these circumstances, I encourage parents to seek permission first and abide by your teen's response. For example, Jim Bower passed his daughter Emily's bedroom door one night and overheard her grumbling to herself about how there was too much to consider when deciding on a college major. He backed up and knocked on her open door.

"Hey, Sweetheart. You sound swamped."

"That's an understatement," Emily sighed.

"Data overload?"

"Uh, huh. Why does the college want to know my anticipated major when I haven't even got there yet? Isn't that what the first two years of coursework are all about?" Emily leaned back in her desk chair and dejectedly tossed her pen toward the desk.

Jim moved near his daughter and gently put his hands on her shoulders as she sat somberly. "Well, Em, I have some thoughts about your dilemma. Do you want to hear them?"

"Sure."

In this vignette, Emily's dad observed her distress. He comforted her with active listening and a soft touch. He listened to her frustrations. He asked permission to give her some ideas.

Using this consultant's format affords you the greatest opportunity for your counsel to be gratefully received. An added benefit is that your relationship with your adult child moves toward becoming an emotionally intimate, close friendship. You will always be their mom or dad, but becoming a good friend is mutually beneficial for a lifetime.

SUMMARY

The attainment of responsible freedom by your teen or young adult is the capstone of your Christ-centered parenting. Our goal is to launch responsible, independent individuals into their adulthood. Shepherding your teen toward that goal requires your implementing the parenting principle of responsible freedom. As the reins of your teens lives are passed from you to them, you have helped them attain a healthy personal identity, and a foundation for autonomy, integrity, responsibility, and trust. They, then, are equipped to pursue positive attention through accomplishment, healthy choices, and successful ventures.

By using your Christ-centered parenting tools, such as active listening, clarification, positive reinforcement, and topical clarity, you promote identity stage development. Such measures as The Talk, developing a collaborative effort by providing accountability and oversight, and moving toward consultative parenting help you in the shepherding process. While it will inevitably be a bumpy ride, the destination of jointly meaningful, mutual friendship as adults is worth the ride.

Lord, help us to hang on as we undertake the most important task for which we are so utterly unprepared. We accept your gracious, and daunting, gift of parenting our teens and shepherding them into productive adulthood. We accept your counsel, as you are always only a prayer away. Help us to use your counsel wisely in our providing wise counsel to our growing teens. Help us to embrace the collaborative effort needed to provide our teen responsible freedom. Help us to be the encourager when he strays, and the role model to whom she looks as she sizes up how to be an adult. Give us safe passage through the portal to responsible, independent adulthood for our children. Amen

Appendix One
Active Listening

Rationale

As a communication tool, active listening is the lifeblood of healthy relationship and communication. In effective, Christ-centered parenting, active listening your child is your educated guess of what she is feeling at the moment. It is a concerted effort to focus on her words, her feelings, and her intent to share something with you.

Many parents (and children/teens) don't listen much at all. In conversation, one is talking and the other is preparing to talk (or rebut). You have a lot of directional conversation with your child. You ask questions and give direction. Active listening, however, is the heart of your efforts to connect with her in helping her solve problems. When you active listen well, she knows you understand. You are with her emotionally. It doesn't mean that you have answers or that the conversation leads to her problem being solved. However, effective active listening results in that "Kodak moment" when she says, "Thanks, Dad, for listening." Or "I know you really understand, Mom. That means a lot to me."

Being An Active Listener

The heart of active listening is simply hearing what your child is saying and responding with variations of "You feel…" The beauty of active listening is that, by your efforts, you are right when you are on the mark, and you are right when you are off the mark.

For example, you hear your child out about a peer problem at school. After her few explanatory sentences, you offer, "You feel hurt when that happens." She looks oddly at you and replies, "No, Daddy, I'm angry."

While it's clear that you missed the mark, your effort and response gave your child opportunity to clarify what she was feeling. Of course, you try to hit the mark frequently, and she beams at you because "you so get me."

Try beginning every response in conversation with your child with "you feel…" and see how long the talk lasts. Everybody gets bored with repetition, so vary your active listening with the following options:

PASSIVE LISTENING. Give your child your undivided, focused attention. Maintain good eye contact. Looking directly at her conveys the importance of her words to you. Lean a little forward in your chair, conveying intensity to your listening.

NON-COMMITTAL RESPONSES. This is what shrinks are famous for. When used sparingly and strategically, however, they are spacers that encourage your child to continue. Such comments as, "Uh huh," "Wow!" "Hmmm," all say nondirectively to her that you are right with her and you encourage her to continue.

ENCOURAGING DIRECTIVE RESPONSES. These are brief comments or questions that help her explore her feelings more thoroughly. For example, you might say, "Tell me more," or, "What was that like for you?"

ACTIVE LISTENING. Beyond "You feel…," your listening to your child is active when you are searching for and replaying the feelings you hear from her. Such expanded active listening would include comments like, "That must have been hard for you." "Oh, boy. What fun!!" "Did that make you feel betrayed?" or, "You sound like you were really excited."

Cautionary Notes

1. Don't judge, evaluate or criticize your child if your intent is to active listen. These errors invalidate her and convey the hidden message that her words are unimportant.

2. Don't provide your solutions to her problems. This error minimizes her efforts and conveys the hidden message that she is too stupid to figure out a viable solution herself.

3. When you think your child has talked out all of her feelings on the subject, it is then okay to ASK PERMISSION to share your thoughts and ideas about her dilemma. Asking permission conveys your respect for her abilities to solve her problems and also gives you opportunity to provide wise counsel. Of course, by your asking permission, be prepared for her to decline, and hold your tongue, further conveying your respect.

The Listening-Sharing Exercise

Rationale

Listening and sharing are two of the most important communication tools in any family and healthy relationship. It is by listening with your heart that you encourage emotional intimacy with your spouse and children. It is by sharing from your soul that you allow yourself to be vulnerable. Mutual vulnerability in shared experiences builds trust and increases relational bonding. A formula for healthy relationship is the following:

$$\frac{\text{I}}{\text{T}} = \underline{\text{R}} + \underline{\text{V}}, \text{ or, } \underline{\text{Intimacy}} \text{ develops by taking } \underline{\text{Risks}} \text{ and allowing} \\ \text{yourself to be } \underline{\text{Vulnerable}} \text{ with another, over } \underline{\text{Time}}$$

The Listening-Sharing Exercise provides a vehicle for practicing emotional intimacy, for working out issues, and for building trust in your relationships.

Procedures

First, with your spouse or child, agree on a 30-minute segment of time where you can complete the exercise without interruption. Make an appointment with each other. Assure that there will be privacy. Avoid interruptions by telephone, television, computer, blackberry, Gameboy, PlayStation, newspaper, or other distractions.

Then decide on your joint topic. At first, I encourage a "starter" topic that is safe, unthreatening for either of you, and yet informative. Often I encourage clients to talk about three positive feelings you each had outside of your time with the other. This topic is safe because you are talking about positive feelings. It is unthreatening because it is about a time outside of your experience with the other. It is informative when you share something that the other is unlikely to know much about.

As you practice the Listening-Sharing Exercise over time, you can use the sequence to tackle hotter topics and to problem solve. It's important at first, however, to get used to using active listening with each other and to practice the undivided attention needed to take on more volatile topics.

Next, you decide who goes first. That person is the Talker. The other is the Listener. After initial roles are agreed upon, begin the 30-minute exercise. Time allocations are as follow:

FOR TEN MINUTES. Talker, share your feelings and experiences on topic. Talk for the full ten minutes. Elaborate on your experiences on topic. Listener, you get the hard part. Listen with your heart. That is, search for the Talker's feelings within the words. Empathize, encourage, and listen intently. You get to practice your active listening.

FOR FIVE MINUTES. Share with each other your experience in your roles. What was it like to "have the floor" and talk for ten full minutes? Did you have trouble filling the time allotment? Were your Listener's comments helpful to you? Listener, how hard was it for you to avoid the "Don'ts?" Did you avoid giving solutions, interjecting off topic? Did you stay interested and involved for the whole ten minutes?

FOR TEN MINUTES. Part two is the same as part one, except now the part one Talker is the part two Listener and the part one Listener is the part two Talker. Talker, find your own experience to share. Be thorough and very descriptive. Listener, use the Active Listening tools and avoid the "Don'ts."

FOR FIVE MINUTES. The half hour exercise is concluded with the second sharing of your experiences in the exercise now that the initial roles have been reversed. Did you like better being the Talker or the Listener? Can you see how this kind of exchange can be helpful in solving problems? In conflict resolution? In working out compromises? Can you imagine bonding closer emotionally with each other by using these listening-sharing tools?

Therapeutic Impact

Having completed and felt good about this "safe topic" listening-sharing experience, you can now plan scheduled times together to repeat the exercise, but with harder topics. Any time you have a beef with the other, flip into listening-sharing mode to help you get through it. After you feel confident with these communication tools, any of you in the family can "call a session" with any other with whom you have a beef.

With confidence, using these tools becomes second nature and an integral part of most every conversation in the family when you are working on the relationships. The 30-minute time frame and structured roles are less important than simply using the tools in focused conversation. Less formally, then, the conversations will be more give and take, but with each being more aware of the other's feelings and both of you joining forces to work on problems.

These tools can be a part of a spouse date night, or a family game night. They also are helpful after asking the "How was your day, dear?" question, as you come home from work or school. They are very effective in bringing the defensive walls down on relationship issues.

Appendix Two
Feeling and Sharing Words

Review the following list of feeling words and phrases. One of the keys to effective active listening is to vary your response and to use synonyms and unique phrases to help the speaker capture what he is feeling.

Competence/Strength

convinced you can	confident	sense of accomplishment	daring
sense of mastery	powerful	feeling one's oats	effective
potent	courageous	sure	sense of conviction
resolute	determined	trust in yourself	self-reliant
strong	influential	sharp	able
brave	impressive	adequate	firm
forceful	inspired	capable	on top of it
successful	secure	can cope	important
in charge	in control	up to it	ready

well-equipped	committed	equal to it	skillful

Happiness/Satisfaction

elated	superb	joyful	cheerful
ecstatic	on cloud nine	happy	organized
	elevated		
serene	calm	lighthearted	wonderful
fantastic	splendid	glowing	jolly
exhalant	jubilant	neat	glad
terrific	euphoric	fine	pleased
delighted	marvelous	good	contented
excited	enthusiastic	hopeful	mellow
thrilled	great	satisfied	gratified
super	in high spirits	tranquil	on top of the world
	fulfilled		

Caring/Love

adore	loving	respect	admire
infatuated	enamored	concern for	taken with
cherish	idolize	turned on	trust
worship	attached to	close	esteem
devoted to	hit it off	value	tenderness toward
affection for	hold dear	warm toward	friendly
prize	caring	like	positive toward
fond of	regard	accept	

Depression/Discouragement

anguished	in despair	distressed	downcast
dreadful	miserable	sorrowful	demoralized
dejected	disheartened	pessimistic	tearful
rotten	awful	weepy	down in the dumps
horrible	terrible	deflated	blue

hopeless	gloomy	lost	melancholy
dismal	bleak	in the doldrums	lousy
depressed	despondent	kaput down	unhappy
grieved	grim	bad	low
brokenhearted	forlorn	disappointed	blah
below par	sad		

Inadequacy/Helplessness

utterly	worthless	unfit	like a klutz
good for nothing	washed up	awkward	deficient
powerless	helpless	unable	incapable
impotent	crippled	small	insignificant
inferior	emasculated	like a wimp	unimportant
useless	finished	over the hill	incomplete
like a failure	impaired	immobilized	like a puppet
inadequate	whipped	at the mercy of	inhibited
defeated	stupid	insecure	lacking confidence
incompetent	puny	unsure of self	uncertain
inept	clumsy	weak	inefficient
overwhelmed	ineffective	lacking	

Appendix Three
Leads for Empathic Responses

Could it be that…?

I'm not sure if I'm with you, but…

Correct me if I'm wrong. I'm sensing…

Maybe you feel…

I don't understand. Do you feel…?

Is that what you mean?

Is that the way you feel?

As I get it, you felt…

To me it's almost like…

I'm picking up that you…

You're feeling…

What I guess I'm hearing is…

It appears you feel…

Do you feel…?

Maybe this is a long shot, but…

As I hear it, you…

I get the impression you feel…

The message I'm getting is that…

So, as you see it…

You feel…

I wonder if…

You appear to be…

Perhaps you're feeling…

Sometimes you think…

It seems that you…

What I think I'm hearing is…

Let me see if I'm with, you feel…

If I'm hearing you correctly, you feel…

So, you're feeling…

It sounds as though you're saying…

I wonder if you're saying...

So, from where you sit...

I sense that you're feeling...

Your message seems to be...

What you're saying comes across to me as...

I hear you saying...

Right now you're feeling...

You must have felt...

You convey a sense of...

As I think about what you say, it occurs to me you're feeling...

So, it seems to you...

I gather you're feeling...

Listening to you, it seems as if...

If I'm catching what you're saying...

From what you say, I gather you're feeling...

Appendix Four
Behavior Management Strategies

Rationale

Children are cute, cuddly critters who can be holy terrors at times if allowed. Parents are given to children to guide them, help them develop mentally, emotionally, socially and spiritually, and to launch them as responsible, independent, community-conscious adults. Helping them traverse that rocky, pock-marked road from infancy to adulthood can be scary, yet enticing, dangerous, but engaging, for both you and your child. Any and all tools available to families that help them succeed on this journey should be considered.

Behavior management strategies provide such tools to help your child over the rough spots and to grow. Effective behavior management strategies provide incentive for him, an understandable rationale and context for positive behavior change, and a spirit of ownership and cooperation in making the changes. One such strategy follows.

The Good Kid Chart

The attached Good Kid Chart is an engaging, fun means of helping your child track behavior change over time. Many parents make the mistake of simplifying the process. They tell their child, "If you do good in school between now and your next report card, I'll take you to Disney World." This is not a behavior management strategy. It is doomed to fail because it's one-dimensional. While parents who use this ploy are well intentioned, there are several fatal flaws.

First, the target behavior, do good in school, is vague and over-generalized. If you do not specifically agree on the obtainable, positive goal, then you could be expecting one thing, while your child is working on another.

Second, the time frame for the reward is way too long. While the attention span of children does lengthen as they grow older, even teenagers top out at about two weeks. Report cards are six to nine weeks apart. Children lose interest in even the grandest of goals as the time frame to reward lengthens.

Third, a single reward is easily dismissed by children. When children realize that they've blown it, that they will not get the reward, then they frequently rationalize that they weren't interested in the goal anyway. This rationalization helps children save face and shifts the blame for their failure to the parents, for not providing the "right" reward.

The Good Kid Chart, and the process developed to guarantee successful, positive behavior change, addresses these pitfalls of one dimensional bribery. The following steps will lead your child to embrace the change process and reach their goals.

Step One—Defining Target Behaviors

In creating the Good Kid Chart, you will want to talk about what behavior changes you want your child to make. Then, list these changes in the left-hand column as target behaviors. Be very careful to word your target behaviors in positive terms. Children get confused and do not easily work toward a negative. For example, "Don't hit your sister," becomes "Play nicely with your sister." The result is the same, but the child responds better to the positive context. As a rule of thumb, children under age 10 usually can handle working on no more than three target behaviors at a time. Older children can handle up to five.

Step Two—Develop Content for Posters

After you have agreed on the number and positive wording of the target behaviors, buy three, 17 x 30" posters of different, bright and bold colors. Children are drawn to bold colors. Title the posters: Daily Rewards, Weekly Rewards, and Consequences.

Agree on a time for a family meeting to introduce and explain the Good Kid Chart to the children, give rationale for each target behavior, and have the children join you in creating lists of rewards and consequences. Each poster should have 6-10 items. All items are within your time and financial constraints.

For each poster, have a brainstorming time with your children to encourage their participation. Write down on paper all of their ideas and all of yours, no matter how wild or far out. After everybody is talked out, go back through the list with attention to the do-ability in terms of time and finances.

DAILY REWARDS—These items need to be available to your child right before bedtime each night. After the Good Kid Chart is reviewed and he has met criteria for a reward, give the reward immediately and with great fanfare and verbal praise. Therefore, items on the Daily Reward List need to be readily accessible. For example, some families have included such items as a bedtime snack, staying up an extra fifteen minutes, reaching into a grab bag full of small toys, listening to soft, bedtime music, and so forth. It is important that you accept some of your child's ideas, as well as offering your own for the list.

WEEKLY REWARDS—These items become available at the conclusion of the week on the Good Kit Chart. They are more expensive and time-consuming because they acknowledge that your child has strung together several good days in a row. He's beginning to make a good and lasting change. However, overall time and financial constraints still apply. Usually, children can pick one item from the Weekly Reward List on Fridays, as the reward options are greater then. For example, some families have included such list items as having a sleepover, putting together a popcorn and movie DVD night, developing a play date, going out to dinner (Chuck E. Cheese?), and so forth. Longer term rewards, such as that trip to Disney World, are not included on these lists. Do not put any item on either list that you would not let your child pick.

CONSEQUENCES—This third poster is also brainstormed, giving your child opportunity to contribute. Interestingly, most children are usually harder on themselves than are their parents on them. Having him add to the list, and subsequently pick his own consequence when one is required, increases his accountability and ownership for his actions. When you simply decide on the consequence, your child can dismiss it by rationalizing that mama is "just being mean."

However, when your child picks from a set list, some items of which he actually put on the list, he is more likely to accept that he screwed up and learn from his negative behavior. On this third poster, some consequences might include restriction, a pop on the bottom, loss of privilege, sitting in a corner, designated time out, and so forth.

Actually, two levels of consequence exist. First, it a consequence for your child to not earn a sticker for the Good Kid Chart. Second, if he "loses it," then he doesn't get the sticker AND he has to choose a consequence from the poster list. If he refuses to pick, the parent can simply pick for him. For example, if "playing nicely with your sister" is a target behavior, and he attacks her for some reason, then he both loses the sticker for that day and also gets a consequence.

Whenever your child does not earn a sticker, or gets a consequence, be sad and empathize with him. For example, you might comment, "I know you wanted to earn that sticker today. I'm sorry you didn't quite get it. You're working hard, though, and I hope you earn it tomorrow." When he has to pick a consequence, use your active listening with such comments as, "I'm sorry you got in trouble. Accepting that you made a bad choice is difficult. I hope you choose more wisely next time so you don't have to go back to the consequence poster."

Step Three—Develop a Baseline for Reward

After all is said and done, pick a starting day to begin using the Good Kid Chart. Put the chart and posters up in a conspicuous place (bedroom, kitchen, family room). Be excited about the system, positive about how you worked on it together, and eager to see how it works.

For the first week, use the Good Kid Chart WITHOUT REWARD OR CONSEQUENCE. This becomes the baseline measure to see how well your child adjusts to this new system. It also gives you a starting point for rewards and consequences. Does he average one, two, or three stickers per day even without getting a reward? How many stickers does he earn for the week?

After this week, he has to at least match his daily average to earn a reward for the day. He has to get his weekly average plus one more each week to earn a reward for the week. This incentive assures continuity and consistency in helping him develop new positive habits.

Step Four—Use of the Good Kid Chart

Before getting started, ask your child how he would like to use the chart. Does he want smiley faces, stickers, or check marks in the circles? Let him choose and let him affix the sticker or mark ONLY IF HE EARNS IT. Some systems suggest smiley faces for success and frowny faces for failure. I do not like to highlight failure. Missing the mark is implied when the circle is empty.

Step Five—Praise Success

Being excited for him and celebrating your child's success is as rewarding for him as any prize he might pick from the poster lists. Set a positive tone. Use what is called presuppositional phrasing when you talk to him about his success. Such wording presupposes positive outcome. For example, you might ask, "Which prize do you think you will pick when you rack up all those smiley faces?" The focus is not on "if" but rather on "when," not on "you can, or might" but rather on "you will."

When your child reaches criteria daily for 2-3 weeks, make a special occasion to acknowledge his efforts and success. Some parents have celebrated success with cupcakes and candles, a special meal, or a surprise not on either reward poster. After he achieves this kind of consistent success, you can remove that target behavior from the Good Kid Chart. He no longer needs to work on that one because he has mastered it. You can, however, talk with him about starting work on a new behavior to replace the mastered one.

Step Six—Chart and Poster Revision

An effective behavior management system is fluid. It allows for "do-overs." If he is not motivated by the items on either reward poster, then go back to the drawing board. Have another family meeting to re-vamp the lists. If he does not achieve smiley faces for a particular target behavior consistently, go back to the drawing board. Have a family meeting to make sure he understands what is expected of him. Make crystal clear the positive behavior he is working on. If he continues to have difficulty, scale down your expectations by either shortening the time frame within which he can earn a sticker, or by breaking down the target behavior into smaller chunks for success.

NOTE: The Good Kid Chart is not meant to be used to keep up with chores or school grades. These may be separate checklists or goal sheets for completion. Typically, chores are completed without extra compensation and not as contingency for allowance. Chore completion is acknowledgement by all that you are a family and that the load needs to be shared. Good grades are your child's way of demonstrating maturity and responsibility for learning.

However, you can negotiate with your children and contract work for pay outside of the normal chores. You can also reward him with money for grades, as extra incentive.

The Good Kid Chart is a tool for behavior management and to be used when your child's behavior is causing undue hardship for himself or others.

GOOD KID CHART

TARGET BEHAVIORS | SUN | MON | TUE | WED | THUR | FRI | SAT

CONTRACT BETWEEN: _____

DIRECTIONS: AT THE END OF THE DAY, DRAW IN A STAR OR A CHECK MARK IF THE GOAL WAS ACHIEVED AND LEAVE IT BLANK IF IT WASN'T.

Appendix Five
The Nurturing-Holding Procedure

Rationale: There are times, albeit infrequent and more so with toddlers and young children, when your child is physically out of control. He's not getting his way and he's throwing a fit! She wants to do one thing and you want her to do another. Does she say, "yes, Ma'am," and comply? No. She falls down wailing and flailing in a full-blown temper tantrum. What's a parent to do?

Your options are several. You could be embarrassed, especially if he gets out of control in public, like the grocery store. In such cases, typically you ask him nicely to please keep it down. People are staring. You bargain with him, bribe him, to be quiet. This bargaining is in the form of, "If you just can be quiet and cooperative so I can finish this chore, then I will get you what you want."

You could also fly off the handle and match your child's temper tantrum with one of your own. I remember hearing as a child, "If you're going to cry, I'll give you something to cry about." This option would include out-yelling her and popping her bottom to assure she knows who's the boss, who's more powerful. The downside of this option is your running the risk of abusing your child and coming to the attention of the authorities.

Either of these options is lose-lose. Each is about control and dominance. In Christ-centered parenting, control and dominance lead to disaster. When you minimize the fit and bargain with your child, he seems to win. He learns that, if he ramps up his response, he gets what he wants. When you match her temper tantrum with one of your own, you win, because you are bigger and can be more forceful. She only learns to keep her mouth shut; she resents you for bullying her; and you control her by her fear of you.

The Nurturing-Holding Procedure (NHP) is a third option for extreme cases of out-of-control behavior by your child. The NHP is a calm but firm physical restraint of your child. You identify your child's behavior as out of control and then calmly convey your confidence that he can get himself back in control, and that you are going to help him by restraining him and giving him time to regain control of himself.

The NHP is a firm, parent-in-charge response that teaches him that he is not going to get his way by throwing a fit. It also is a love/respect-based parenting strategy that gives her responsibility for her actions and encourages her compliance to your expectations without fearing you.

Procedure: The NHP is equally a physical and a verbal response to your child's out-of-control behavior. When a tantrum includes hitting others, destroying property, and putting himself or others in danger of harm, then the NHP is a useful parental response that will end your child's tantrum. The benefits of the NHP are immediate and frequently long lasting. After having successfully brought her out of tantrum behavior, you often only have to remind your child that she is getting out of control. Then ask her if she wants you to control her until she can get herself back in control.

Physical Restraint: At the first signs of tantrum, and you decide that your child is not able to restrain himself, tell him that you are going to physically control him until he can get himself back in control.

1. Hold him from behind, in either a standing or sitting position. Wrap your arms around his body, holding his wrists and crossing his and your arms in front of him. Snugly hold this position with your arms roughly at your child's waist. This position helps you avoid his biting you.

2. If he is kicking as well, wrap your legs around his legs and sit down on a chair or the floor to restrain him from kicking out as best as possible.

3. Keep your head back and away from his head, as many such restrained children will try to head butt if their arms and legs are secure.

Verbal Soothing/Reassurance: Even after she is physically restrained, your child will likely continue to strain to get away. She will beg and plead. She will tell you that you are hurting her. She may call you every name in the book. These words are her verbal tantrum and only code for "I don't like what's happening to me. I'm angry. I'm scared. I'm out of control."

As you continue to physically restrain her, begin verbal soothing and reassurance.

1. Slow your breathing. Your bodies are entwined, so your slower breathing will encourage her slower breathing and calming down. You can also add verbally, "Breathe. Breathe deeper. Deep, calming breaths."

2. Say to her, "Stop it. Stop it. Come on. I know you can do it. Calm yourself down."

3. Reassure her that you are only going to control her as long as she is not able to control herself. Define for her that yelling, straining, kicking, hurting or trying to hurt herself or others is evidence that she is still not yet in control of herself. Add, paradoxically, "You are in charge here, sweetheart. You will tell me by your actions when you are getting yourself back in control. You will tell me by your actions when to loosen up; when you are ready to be back in control of yourself."

4. As she calms down, stops fighting you and straining to get loose, reassure her. "Look at you. Look at how great you are doing. You are beginning to get yourself back in control. Good job. I'm so proud of you. Are you ready for me to let go?"

5. Older children can pretend to be in control and calmed down, but will ramp up after giving you assurance that they are ready for you to let go. If that happens, simply reassert your physical restraint with assuring comment, "Oops! I guess you were not as ready as you thought in getting

yourself back in control. That's okay. I will hold on to you for as long as you need for me to. Let me know when you are ready again."

Debriefing: After your child has calmed down and regained control, plan to talk to him about the event. Some children are embarrassed by their behavior and really don't want to talk about it right away. That's okay. Other children are exhausted and just want something light to eat and go to bed. That's okay.

If not right away, at least mark the time within the next couple of hours or day that you will sit down together to review and to figure out how to avoid such drastic parenting in the future. This is the time to understand your child's feelings and motivations in acting out. It is also the time to reinforce your expectations of his behavior and his problem-solving abilities. Make clear to him that any physical harm to people or property, any shouting match, any extreme attitude are unacceptable. You are a Christ-centered family who are committed to loving each other unconditionally and to raising your children up in the ways of the Lord.

Benefits of Utilizing the NHP: The NHP has obvious benefits in immediately stopping any further harm to person or property. Additionally, it gives a definitive answer to the question, "Who's in charge?" Further, effective use of the NHP, with both physical restraint and verbal calming/reassurance, relaxes your child. With his straining to break free, he soon wears out. A useful relaxation technique is to alternatively tense and relax muscle groups. The NHP promotes this relaxation process.

Finally, the NHP is a demonstrative affirmation of your unconditional love for your child. Parents often tell children during an NHP, "I love you so much that I'm going to keep holding on to you and controlling you until you can control yourself. You're not loving you when you are out of control. It's okay. I'll love you for both of us and you will love yourself again soon enough."

A Final Note: The NHP is best used in the privacy of your home and within earshot of only supportive, loving family members. Children who are being physically restrained against their will often cry foul and attempt to enlist support and collusion from family, friends, and even strangers. Especially children who are older than 5 will try to even the power differential by accusing you of child abuse.

Also, just like spanking, the NHP is not a good option for an angry parent. Our children often know what we are feeling even before we know. They will benefit from your calm resolve and loving reassurance. You really can't pull that off if, underneath, you are angry and your goal is a power play to show your child who is the boss.

Finally, where there is a possibility of extreme acting out in public, such as when grocery shopping or at the mall, it is crucial for parents to plan ahead. Such outings are a growing experience for your child and a teaching opportunity for you. If at all possible, both parents go, or one parent and a close, adult friend. Prompt a good response from your son by reminding him of the rules. If he has done well on previous outings, reinforce how well he did before and ask if he can do as well today. His response becomes a verbal contract and a reference point for you as the outing unfolds.

If the outing begins to go poorly, you could use the NHP to physically restrain your child, but I would advise against it. Your parenting would draw a crowd, no matter how good your intentions or technique.

Instead, with prompting and planning, simply hold your child firmly, advise him that his behavior is unacceptable, and then immediately leave, carrying your child with you. Let your spouse or friend continue the outing with the other children or alone to complete the shopping list. Despite whatever protest from your child, go the car and go home.

When children know that you are serious, often their acting out stops, they become penitent, and they plead to continue the outing. Be firm that the outing is over for your child. Consequent with empathy by telling him that you hope he makes wiser choices next time so his outing can continue, and then he can have the fun, toy, or surprise you had hoped to give him this time.

Having your spouse or friend complete the outing is equally important for two reasons. First, you want to accomplish your task. Second, you don't want to give your child the power to disrupt the whole family/errand process.

Practice Activity: Take a moment to talk about the NHP. How well do you think it could be implemented in your family? When was there a time in the past where this procedure could have come in handy? How do you think your child would have responded to it?

Practice the NHP with the cooperation of your child. Get feedback about how it feels both to control and to be controlled. Have your child test your physical restraining abilities by trying to get himself free.

Appendix Six
Diet or Weight Management?

Rationale

Are you overweight? By how much? How do you know what your ideal body weight is? How do you feel? Is your body cooperating at your size, or is it breaking down and in revolt?

These are hard questions that confront people who want to be healthy. Weight loss needs to be a whole lot more about how your body is working, or not working, for you than about how you look and whether your clothes still fit you. After deciding to lose weight, you then want to compare the benefits of dieting to weight management. Healthy weight loss that stays off is a product of ongoing weight management.

Alcoholics refer to their disease as alcoholism. There is a two-part recovery process. First, stop drinking alcohol. Second, make lifestyle changes that increase the likelihood that you will never drink again. Recovering alcoholics refer to this part as "the ism." When an active alcoholic commits to both parts of the recovery, he attains abstinence. While this implies never drinking again, recovering alcoholics will tell you they are not going to drink "for today." The One Day At A Time philosophy of recovery sustains an alcoholic and reminds him that he is one drink away from relapse.

Although not all obese people are food addicts, weight management and alcoholism recovery have a lot in common. Of course, abstinence is not a part of weight management. The body will not allow you to starve yourself by never eating again. And yet, as you commit to a weight management program, make lifestyle changes that promote healthy choices, and take it one day at a time, your unhealthy weight comes off gradually and stays off. You reach your goal weight.

Defining Goal Weight

Four factors go into calculating your goal weight: your height, weight, bone structure, and body mass index, or BMI. Insurance companies use height and bone structure to determine average range of weight. Bone structure is simply measured as large, medium, or small-boned by circling your wrist with your thumb and second finger. If your fingers do not meet, you are large-boned. If they meet, you are medium-boned. If they overlap, you are small-boned. Calculation of your BMI is more complicated. This is the formula:

Weight divided by height squared, then multiplied by 704

Or

Weight times .45, divided by height times .024 squared

A normal BMI is between 18.5 and 24.9; underweight is less than 18.5, while overweight is between 25 and 29.9. Obesity is defined as being 25% over your average range of weight, or having a BMI over 30. Morbid obesity, indicating a life threatening condition, is defined as being 50% over your average range of weight or having a BMI over 40. Where obesity has compromised several medical systems, morbidity increases.

Obesity is Never The Only Problem

The more body systems that are affected by your excessive weight, the greater the impact of your obesity. Often, people who are excessively overweight are also diabetic, have high blood pressure, high cholesterol, heart problems, and breathing problems. They also frequently have acid reflux and other gastrointestinal problems. They might have difficulty holding their bladder, difficulty sleeping, and suffer from chronic muscle and joint pain. They might have arthritis in their bones as well as joints, heel spurs, and their body may have trouble getting rid of excessive water. While all of these conditions can come about from other medical problems, if you are excessively overweight, you have a greater likelihood of having these and other difficulties.

In addition to the physical issues, psychological issues plague people who are excessively overweight. Such obese people wrestle with embarrassment, humiliation, and shame. Over time, and without psychological help, these issues lead to self-hatred, self-contempt, depression, damaged self-esteem, and social withdrawal. Gradually, their worlds become smaller and smaller as they get bigger and bigger in size.

The Seduction of Dieting—Dieting Is Not The Answer!

God forbid you would ever have an affair. If you did fall to that temptation, the affair would be passionate, illicit, and short-termed. Lovers are looking for a quick fix to their emptiness. They want the excitement without the commitment. The percentages of divorce go way up, when the marriage is the product of mutual infidelity. There is no shortcut to the completion and fullness of a healthy marriage. It takes hard work, continual assessment of feelings, commitment through the hard times, and an on-going communication. An affair gives you none of these things.

Dieting is like having an affair. There is an initial allure, many promises to yourself, and good intentions. The quick fix to weight loss works no better for the dieter than the affair does for the adulterer. Serial adultery leads to more emptiness. Chronic dieting dooms most people to failure to reach their goal weight. In fact, many people who stop dieting, out of frustration, find the lost weight coming back, and then they gain more weight! Dieting creates a state of deprivation and semi-starvation, leading to meal skipping, food preoccupation, cravings, and then over-eating just to try to make yourself feel better. Go figure.

Effective Weight Management

Don't just lose the weight. Keep it off. This works by putting your whole mind, body, and spirit into the weight management process. You cannot think or pray yourself to your goal weight. The cognitive and spiritual dimensions follow the hard work of the physical dimension. Choosing to lose weight and keep it off requires that losing weight becomes your single-most important priority in your life.

Start by calculating your reasonable goal weight, given your age, height, bone structure, and body mass index. Crunch the numbers to find your goal weight. Next, use graph paper to chart your weight on a daily basis. The chart becomes your accountability partner, your guide to daily activities, and your source of pride in accomplishment even in the small amounts of weight loss that start the process. When you have lots of weight to lose, you won't notice a pound or two loss from one day to the next unless you mark it out, literally, on the graph paper.

Weigh yourself daily, at roughly the same time of the day, and chart your weight. We vary in weight from three to five pounds within a twenty-four hour period of time, so it is helpful to weigh yourself each morning after your bathroom routine and before breakfast. This will give you the most honest measure.

Next, there is no substitute for calorie counting. Nutritionists will tell you that weight gain is most likely when your daily count exceeds 3000 calories. Weight loss is possible when you consume 2000-3000 calories per day, with moderate exercise. Consuming less than 1200 calories per day results in feelings of starvation, excessive hunger, and becomes counter-productive. Not eating enough each day will lead to medical problems and may trigger binge eating.

Several "tips" aid in making your calorie intake goals. Many studies encourage drinking water as your only beverage throughout the day. On average, this becomes 6-8, 8 oz. glasses of water daily. Also, eat your usual three meals per day, but reduce portions to stay within your calorie limits. Trick your mind by putting your meal on a smaller plate! Make sure your meals are balanced and nutritional.

Also, stick to meals only. Avoid the "3 S's," that is, avoid seconds, snacks, and scraps. I grew up with a mother who reminded me of all those starving children in India, as a way of guilting me into cleaning my plate. I ate everything on my plate all right. As I grew up and had my own family, I cleaned my plate and all the others around the family dinner table as well. I still, however, haven't figured out how my plate-cleaning behavior helped all those starving children in India! Sticking only to three meals and avoiding incidental eating will keep you in your calorie goal range.

Finally, exercising is the regulator for your weight management program. It also is the gateway to the mind and spirit dimensions of weight control. If you "fudge" (pun intended) on your calorie intake, more exercise will burn off the excess calories. Exercise begins where your body allows. If you are able to walk, then walk. If you can power walk, then step it up. If you have resources to swim, the buoyancy makes the exercise easier, and swimming strokes involve all the body muscles at once, giving you a more complete workout.

If you have access to a stepper, stationary bike, or other exercise equipment or free weights, work your way up to a good workout. At whatever level of exercise, repetitive motion for twenty minutes will purge hour cardiovascular system and increase your metabolism. This means that stored fat will begin to burn off.

For weight management purposes, ideally, a good workout includes twenty minutes to get your cardiovascular system pumping and forty minutes of concentrated, repetitive motion against whatever resistance you can tolerate. The saying "no pain, no gain," is actually true. Of course, begin slowly and get cleared by your physician for your particular exercise regimen before getting started.

Use your weight chart to monitor your success. As a rule of thumb, if your weight stays the same for three days, or whenever your weight goes up, review your previous day's weight management efforts. You will likely find the error of your ways. Then redouble your efforts for today to stay the course. Keep your calorie intake within weight loss parameters, but maybe add more exercise. Review your intake. Was it that glass of iced tea you had with lunch yesterday? Did you eat after dinner last night? Did that fudge sundae blow a hole in your calorie count? Keeping the weight chart daily keeps you focused and helps you catch the "oops" before the damage is so great that you feel defeated.

Add Mind and Spirit

What you tell yourself throughout your weight loss and subsequent management sets the tone for success. Because of gender metabolism, women are successful in losing weight and keeping it off if you lose between 1and 3 pounds per week. Men can keep it off when you lose between 3 and 5 pounds per week. Knowing this, tell yourself to go slow. Don't expect too much too soon. In fact, too much too soon is a sure sign of rebounding to excessive weight gain! Using your mind to control your body impulses allows your weight management to continue productively.

You mind has a set point that regulates food intake and stimulates appetite if you are not eating enough to reach it. Effective weight loss involves changing eating habits, avoiding "comfort food," and maintaining the cognitive willpower to stay the course. Because of the set point in your brain, the first third of your projected weight loss tends to be hard to lose. You are "convincing" the set point to let go. The middle third tends to fly off, as you achieve mind over matter. The last third of your weight loss is also very hard to achieve, as you are "reassuring" the set point to lower its expectations and maintain a smaller size.

How you feel about yourself throughout your weight loss and subsequent management is a produce of your spirit. Pray through your weight loss. Paul wrote about your body being a temple to the Lord. Make it hallow by making it fit and trim. Additionally, as you monitor your feelings throughout your weight management efforts, your will reinforce your success. Feeling lighter, more comfortable, better able to fit into your clothes, into your social life, all lead to healthier self-acceptance, higher self-esteem, and more self-confidence.

Having an outlet for your feelings will make you less likely to "eat your feelings," which is what comfort food is all about. Journaling daily helps you express what you are feeling. Have your feelings in a healthy, productive way. Exercising regularly releases endorphins in your brain, which help you feel better, more fulfilled, and less stressed. Anger, in any form, is the source of negative energy and very counterproductive to healthy weight management. When you become angry, feel it, and look for healthy, productive ways to release it. Talking it out, exercising, or writing it out are all healthy releases for anger. Stuffing anger in particular and feelings in general leads to stuffing food. Maintaining a positive spirit leads to success in weight management.

Appendix Seven
Therapeutic Journaling

Rationale

As children and teens many of us kept journals. We called them "diaries." Some parents promote journaling by buying their child a Dear Diary book of blank pages, complete with a lock and key to reinforce the power and privacy of journaling. Typically, such journals are topical or relational. Many a teenage girl fantasizes about "that cute boy who sits two rows up and one over in front of me in math class." Boys often write stories about their athletic exploits, or they take on the persona of a superhero or action figure. People make these journal entries periodically, when they are in the mood, or when they want to record an event or an intense situation. Such topical or relational journals have their place, and are a good place to vent feelings but they are not therapeutic.

Therapeutic journals are designed to provide a reference and a foundation for everyday healing and stress release. You are the main character in your journal. You chronicle your daily events and your thoughts and feelings about them. The act of journaling becomes second nature to you, just as brushing your teeth or using the bathroom before going to bed each night. A therapeutic journal, over time, provides a vehicle for healing, for noticing your life and the activities that promote or detract from your health. It is a source of perspective, hope, and change.

Procedure

Dedicate a new, clean notebook or pad for the purpose of journaling. Opening a pass protected file on your computer would also work, but I find that the hard copy version is more therapeutic and not as easily deleted.

Begin your journal entries with today's date. Some people simply launch into the day's events from there. Others find added value by making each journal entry a letter to God. If you choose the latter, don't get all flowery, with the King James "thee's and thou's." It's just you and God, so write it because you are writing to a dear and trusted friend. Go through your day's events and your feelings about those events. You don't want any one journal entry to be much longer than a standard notebook page, so you won't be able to include all of the day's events.

Focus on your highlights and lowlights. Try to avoid editorial comment about people and places, as these can be distracting to the therapeutic value of journaling. With each recorded event, think of how or why it happened and also write your feelings before, during, and after the event.

After completing your journal entry, rank the day on a scale of 1 to 10. If your journal is generic, your rankings define relatively bad days (1) from good days (10). However, the process can be tailored to address specific issues in your life as well. The rankings could measure how depressed, anxious, or stressed you were that day. They could also define your relative success at conquering an addiction, losing weight, or making new friends, for example.

Make your ranking after you write your journal entry. Over the years, I have found that rankings may change by virtue of the journaling process, so write the journal entry and then rank that day.

The best time to journal is right before going to bed. This is a natural break in your day's events. It promotes the value of bringing the day to a close with journaling. It is easily associated with other bedtime routines, and therefore more likely to become a positive habit. When effectively written, journaling should not take longer than ten minutes per night.

Therapeutic Benefits of Journaling

1. It increases your self-worth over time. You are committing to a positive behavior that sheds light on your thoughts and feelings and gives you a forum for perspective and release.

2. It brings definitive closure to the day's events, thereby making it less likely for you to feel overwhelmed. Days don't bleed over to the next when you have "closed the book" on today by journaling.

3. It increases your feelings of personal control. You choose what goes into the journal and what's not worth recording. You see the connection between action and reaction in your daily events. You begin to focus on changing the things over which you have control, rather than putting time and energy into trying to change things over which you have no control.

4. It becomes a repository of tools for living a fulfilling and productive life. Previous entries become reference material for making subsequent decisions to help you continue your journey toward "having life more abundantly" (John 10:10)

5. It becomes a source of ideas for ways to change your feelings for the next day. When you've had a bad day, you can thumb back through your journal entries to find a particularly good day. In re-reading that day's journal entry, you will find something that you can do to increase your ranking for tomorrow.

6. It becomes a track record, and your positive changes are more noticeable over time. Some people even graph their daily rankings to visually appreciate their progress.

7. You become much better at capturing the essence of what you are feeling. You also get really good at noticing subtle differences, shades, or nuances in your feelings. At first you know clearly how a 1 ranking differs from a 10 ranking. With time and practice, you get good at distinguishing a 4

from a 5. Such subtle distinctions promote healing and control over the subtle changes in your feelings.

Journal Spin-offs

Although not therapeutic journaling per se, several forms of therapeutic writing often spin off from the journaling process. They include;

1. "To Do" lists. People naturally feel more organized while journaling. It is likely that the process may lead to keeping a separate list of things to do tomorrow that will enhance your journey. If you write these lists, keep them relatively short, five or less items. Also, actually cross each item off as it is completed. Such a simple act is a literal affirmation of your success and motivates you to go to the next item. It also is helpful to attach a time estimate to each item, so that you can gauge your efforts through the day.

2. Letters. As a part of bringing closure to ended relationships, promoting healing from bad relationships, and providing a context for apology/ forgiveness, therapeutic letters are valuable. I encourage writing two letters, if you intend to actually communicate with the other person. The first letter is written with the knowledge that it is not going to be sent. This "letter not sent" gives you opportunity to put any level of emotional intensity and/or invective that you need to release. It becomes a personal brainstorming session, where you write out everything that comes to mind. The second letter is edited for the purpose of the recipient reading it. The purpose of the letter not sent is changing you. With the letter sent, you hope to change the recipient.

3. Time sensitive goals. This would be a list of objectives to be completed, goals to be reached within a prescribed time frame. Often the goals are listed as;
    a. By one month from now, I will…
    b. By six months from now, I will…
    c. By one year from now, I will…

The purpose of such goal statements is to help you keep the big picture in mind and stay on track. They promote a longer term healing experience.

Getting Started

Tonight would be good. However, while therapeutic journaling works best when it is on-going, give yourself a short period of time, a week or a month, to try it out and see how it feels. Consider this a personal experiment before committing long-term to the process. You can tweak the process to see what works best for you. With consistency it will become a positive habit that will continue to promote your healing journey.

Appendix Eight
Restrictions that Work

Rationale

When older children get in trouble, we often punish them by restriction. Typically, children older than ten should not be spanked, and never by the opposite gender parent. Because they are becoming old enough to use abstract reasoning, it is time for parents to restrict, rather than to spank.

Restriction holds your child accountable for her wrongdoing. She can accept responsibility for making a poor choice, and she can learn from her mistake. Punishment, on the other hand, can be confusing to your child if there is no link to the problem behavior. If your teen stays out past her curfew and you punish her by having her do push-ups, what's the lesson?

Punishment can also harm her self-esteem and will damage her relationship with you. Using a set number of "licks" with a switch, belt, or the hand, at any age, is not only harmful and marginally legal, but also generates fear as the rationale for being good. Restriction is the best measure of discipline, especially for older children and teens.

Types of Restriction

Confinement: Placing your errant son in a time-out chair, or in his room, is a means of limiting his movement. The rule of thumb for time-out is to leave him alone in his time-out space for no more than two minutes for every year of his age. Thus, a 10-year old would have a time-out of no more than twenty minutes.

When using confinement, tell him why he is going into time-out. Be very clear and concrete. "You're a bad little boy," serves no helpful purpose, other than for you to vent your anger. "Hitting mommy with a stick is bad. Never hit anyone with a stick. You could hurt them very much." This example is clear, concrete, concise, and it provides directive and reason.

Typically confinement locations are pretty sparse in terms of distraction. If you send your child to his room, restrict him from using the TV, CD, computer, or other items that would make the confinement more bearable. After his time-out, have him tell you why he's in time-out and how he can avoid future times-out. If he cannot give you a reasonable strategy to avoid future times-out when you get back with him, then give him the correct answer and have him repeat it back to you. When he can repeat it back to you, or offer it voluntarily, without negative attitude, the confinement should end. He can then come out of time-out.

Loss of Privilege: Taking things away from her is loss of privilege. With teenagers in particular, there is often confusion between what is a right and what is a privilege. Food, clothing, and shelter are the rights of teens. Everything else is a privilege. Privilege occurs as a reward for good behavior and for his conforming to your parental expectations. The basic tenet is do good and good things happen. Do bad and good things are lost, for a while.

Privileges controlled by parents include toys, games, cell phones, use of the family car, use of your teen's own car, since it is titled in your name, CD's, DVD's, MP3's, Xbox, and the like. Loss of privilege helps teach your child that his actions have consequences, and that with responsibility comes privilege. If he is acting irresponsibly, then he loses privilege.

You want to restore his lost privileges when you are satisfied that he has learned the lesson by demonstrating consistent responsibility over time, and after he makes amends. While the time frame is inexact, too long a time may generate hopelessness in your child. You lose credibility when he feels hopeless to have his privileges returned. Too long a time and loss of privilege becomes another form of punishment. You want loss of privilege to be a disciplinary learning tool. Too short a time frame may void the lesson and lead to recurring rule violations. If he can do without the privilege, then he might think his crime is worth the punishment.

Continue to talk to your child throughout his loss of privilege and you will get a feel for his sincerity and integrity. Sprinkle active listening into your talks and you both will gain insight as to where this rule-breaking behavior came from in the first place. Depending on the violation, loss of privilege rarely should run more than a day for every year of your child's age.

Restriction: Creating a deprivation of significant magnitude is a restriction. Oftentimes, restriction is the result of confinement and loss of privilege adding up. Restriction is best used for bigger violations, where a life lesson has been lost on her and she needs a viable disciplinary learning tool. Many parents call this "grounding." There are helpful and unhelpful ways to ground your child.

It is unhelpful to ground her for obscure reasons, for an excessive time, or for an indefinite time. If she's "being bad," that's too obscure. If you are so mad that you blurt out that she is grounded "until you're 30," or, "for the rest of the year," that's too excessive. If you conclude that she is grounded "until I say you're off grounding," that's too indefinite.

These unhelpful contexts for grounding can lead to emotional harm to your child. They could also promote a conspiracy among siblings or a manipulation of parents to get around the grounding. Unhelpful grounding is rarely a learning tool that promotes respect for rules and for authority. It also rarely helps develop positive character. Such grounding is merely punishment that helps you feel powerful and provides you a means to vent anger at your child.

Helpful ways to ground start with heartfelt discussion with your child about the difficulty, her response, your perspective, and your hopes for how she can learn from this problem. Out of this discussion comes a clear understanding of what she did and of how the restriction can help her remember to think before acting next time and make better choices.

For example, your daughter brings home a poor school progress report. Getting bad grades is too general and she can dismiss this as your simply being unfair or expecting too much of her. However, if your heartfelt discussion and active listening uncovers the path to bad grades, then you have given her a gift of understanding. You might discover that she had not brought home her agenda, leading to her missed assignments, which she failed to turn in to her teacher. Missing the assignments led to her not having all of the material to study for the tests, which led to low test scores and the poor progress report. Without the discussion, you miss an opportunity to help her connect the dots and appreciate how her actions (or inactions) have consequences.

When you are not specific, too excessive, or indefinite in your grounding, you risk your child simply becoming angrier, feeling more hopeless, and being indignant. If she doesn't know why she's being grounded, and the grounding seems forever, then why should she bother to make any changes? She will just wait you out until you get tired of enforcing the grounding or forget about it. Or worse, she will just go underground, sneak around, and undermine all of your efforts.

A Relational Model for Restriction

Helpful ways to ground children promote a working together by parent and child toward the common goal of learning from the difficulty and getting back in your good graces. It is also helpful to encourage his control over his own destiny.

Punishment is usually thought of in terms related to the penal system. When a child is restricted, he considers himself "in jail." If you relent on his "sentence," he "got a reprieve," "got paroled," or, "got sentence commuted to time served." Unfortunately, some parents use these references as well, even though they promote an adversarial relationship between parent and child. This punitive model serves no useful purpose on your journey of raising independent, responsible adult children.

A more user-friendly model comes from Scripture. In the Old Testament, God is usually portrayed as a distant, but concerned parent who is watching over his Chosen People, the Israelites. The whole idea of monotheism was just taking hold and the Israelites were constantly under extreme influences. When they stepped over the line, the Bible tells of how God held them accountable and exacted *Judgment* on them. This often came in the form of casting them out or inflicting other consequences.

As the Israelites "got it," showed remorse, and were penitent, then God relented and showed them *Compassion*. This is where the consequences are lessened and things begin going better for them. As the story unfolded, and the Jewish faith in one God solidified, the Bible moves into the New Testament, where Jesus Christ is introduced.

With the teachings of Jesus, the people of God are introduced to God's *Mercy*. This is where the consequences are lifted because the people have accepted God's role and developed an on-going, personal relationship with Him. In this more user-friendly relational model of parenting, a child's restriction can progress from Judgment to Compassion to Mercy.

Judgment: Here, after your heartfelt discussion with your child, you tell him what his consequence is. For example, following the poor grades scenario, you might conclude, "Until I can see consistent improvement in your responsibilities to bring your agenda home daily, complete and turn in your homework on time, and study hard for your tests, you will not be able to use your cell phone or leave the house after you get home from school for the next four weeks. This is my judgment. Any questions?"

Compassion: As he accepts your judgment and begins to bring his agenda home, completes and turns in his homework, and gets higher test grades because of his more effective studying, then you have the opportunity to show compassion. You might say, "Wow! I'm impressed that you haven't asked for your cell phone back or tried to go out after school this past week since we talked. This 'B' on your math test shows me that you are really trying. Tell you what. I'm going to show you compassion. Your restriction is now for only three weeks instead of four. You've completed one week already. Only two to go. Good job!"

Mercy: Another week has gone by and your son continues to respect his restriction and work on his grades as you had discussed. At this point, you might say, "Son, what a great job you are doing. I think you have learned something here. What do you think?"

If he is able to convey a positive learning with sincerity, then you might follow with, "You know what? You've got it. I'm going to show you mercy. You've completed two weeks of restriction and I am lifting the rest of it. Good for you. I'm proud of you."

Impact of the Relational Model of Restriction

When using this relational model, I encourage you to actually use the words Judgment, Compassion, and Mercy. These are powerful words that convey both your authority and your Christ-centered parenting. The sequence in this restriction from Judgment to Compassion to Mercy promotes your child's accountability with both cooperation and hope. He can play a role in lessening his consequence by simply conforming to your expectations. The focus of the relational model remains on using restriction as a learning tool, rather than solely as a means of punishment. Your positive parent-child relationship remains secured.

Appendix Nine
Chillin' Out—Developing A Quieting Response

Are Stress, Worry, and Freak-Outs Getting the Best of You?

There may not be a day that goes by where you are free of stress and worry, and where things don't get to you. When these things happen, your body and your mind start working against you, feeding these feelings and making them worse.

How Do You React?

Frequently, with these feelings, your breathing becomes rapid and shallow. Your heart rate will increase to the point that you can feel it beating, even feel like it's beating out of your chest. Your blood pressure will increase as well. When your worries become consistent and ruminative, so that it seems like you can't get the worry off your mind, it's hard to think about anything else. As stress gets worse, fears of being overwhelmed and feelings of hopelessness set in. At the worst, you believe irrationally that there is nothing you can do to change the circumstances and that you are completely out of control. Bummer!!!

What to do? What to do? QRs to the Rescue.

The Quieting Reflex (QR) technique is designed specifically to address these symptoms. Using QRs can bring calm and can help you focus attention back to where you feel more relaxed, more at peace, and more in control.

How Do I Develop QRs?

Practice, practice, practice when your stress is minimal and your circumstances are relatively calm. At first, QRs are conscious deep breathing. The letters begin as a *quieting response*, which, with practice over time, becomes a *quieting reflex*. With practice, QRs become reflexive and unconscious. They are automatically available to you in high stress times as you begin having symptoms of stress.

QRs are a Two-Part Calming Event.

Clinically, QRs are a psychophysiological event for you. The physiological, or body part event, involves changing how you are breathing. Most people, breathing naturally, take about three seconds per respiration (breathing in and out). During a QR, you are consciously deepening your breath, so that it takes about six seconds per respiration.

Try to make your breath even, deep, and consistent. Inhale slowly and fully, until your lungs are completely expanded. Without holding your breath at the top of your intake, immediately and slowly exhale until your breath is completely released. With this slower, deeper breathing pattern, your blood system is working better for you, carrying more oxygen to your brain so you can think more clearly. You are also lowering your heart rate and reducing your blood pressure by breathing more deeply.

The QR is also a psychological event designed to slow your racing thoughts, increase your control, and reduce your stress. As you are breathing deeply, first smile inwardly and with your eyes. Everybody knows how to smile with your mouth. Your eyes?? What is actually happening is that you are changing your focus from what's out there (in the world, in front of you) to what is in here (internally, in your mind). Simply smiling inwardly and with your eyes stops racing thoughts. It focuses your attention on internal events and thereby diminishes the perceived threat of external events which are beyond your control.

Next, be curious about your circumstances and your body function. Worry is fueled by "what if" questions your brain is forming under stress. Calm and comfort is fueled by "I wonder" statements. For example, "What if my heart explodes?" is replaced in your mind by "I wonder when I will notice my heart rate slowing down." The "I wonder" curiosity focus on the positive presuppositions about upcoming events. "What ifs" create tensing, constricting, and withholding sensations in your body. "I wonders" generate relaxing, expanding, and creative sensations.

Finally, while breathing deeply, find a picture in your mind of something that is calming, relaxing, and peaceful. It can be an experience you have had in your life, or one that you imagine would fill the bill. For example, imagine soaking in a hot tub of water. Imagine being curled up in a blanket in front of a crackling fire on a cold winters' night. Imagine walking on the beach and listening to the rhythmic sound of the waves. Imagine being in the presence of the Lord and experiencing his gift of "peace that passes all understanding.

Make it Real for You!

If you have specific situations where you have consistently been stressed, worried, or panicked in the past, and you are using QRs to work on these situations, you need to make it real for you. That is, rather than just think about QRs when you need them, practice them when you don't need them. Rather than rely only on your efforts in the moment to calm down, take time to write down a list of the five most frequently occurring "What ifs." Then counter each "What if" question with a paired "I wonder" statement, complete with a presuppositional phrase that encourages the good thing you want to happen. Also, take time to write down a one-page, five sensory description of your calming, peaceful event, real or imagined.

Give yourself time to practice QRs when not stressed at least 50 times per day. While that seems like a whole lot of time, remember that a QR, both deep breathing and the change in thinking, only lasts about six seconds. Fifty times six seconds is only five minutes of practice per day. Also, QRs are a private event that can occur even in a public place or when surrounded with friends and relatives. Nobody but you knows that you are taking a deeper, more rhythmic breath. Nobody knows your quieting thoughts as you are having them.

With practice you will gradually develop a quieting reflex, and your body will start calming at the slightest hint of stress or upset. Over time, all you will actually notice is that you are breathing more deeply and more rhythmically. The psychological parts of the QR will begin to happen more automatically in response to perceived high stress or upset. With practice of QRs, you will feel more hopeful, more in control, and more calm and relaxed. You will be better able to cope with whatever adversity or difficult life event that presents itself to you.

Say What? A Quick Review.

QR stands for quieting response, which becomes a quieting reflex with practice over time. A QR is a six second, deep breathing respiration, involving roughly six seconds of breathing slowly in and an equal six seconds of breathing slowly out.

During this deeper breathing, focus your thoughts on three things:

1. Smiling inwardly and with your eyes,
2. Being curious about what is happening, changing "what if" questions into "I wonder thoughts, and,
3. Finding and focusing on a positive, calming, relaxing visual image in your mind.

Now, practice chillin' out.

About the Author

Dr. Robinson has over 35 years of clinical experience in conducting psychotherapy with individuals, couples, families, and groups. Jon completed his Ph.D. from the University of Virginia, specializing in child-clinical psychology with minors in ED/LD special education and child development.

He does directive, problem-solving-oriented play therapy with children and cognitive-behavioral psychotherapy with adults. He has helped patients who are suffering from depression, anxiety, trauma, abuse, addiction, and relational distress. Also children who have ADD, ADHD, conduct disorder, autism, Asperger's disorder, learning disorder, and emotional-behavioral problems. He does school consultations with teachers and confers on the placement of children with special education needs.

Jon has been married to his wife Margaret, since 1970. They have two adult children, five grandchildren, and are members and serve in the deacon ministry in their local church.

General References

Cline, F. W. & Fay, J. <u>Parenting with Love and Logic (Updated and Expanded Edition)</u>. Love and Logic Press: Boulder, CO, 2006.

Dobson, J. <u>The New Strong-Willed Child</u>. Tyndale House Publishers: Wheaton, IL, 2007.

Erikson, E. <u>Identity & the Life Cycle</u>. WW Norton & Co: New York, NY, 1994.

Harlow, H.F. The Nature of Love. <u>American Psychologist</u>, Vol. 13(12), 673-685, December 1958.

Hazen, B. S. <u>If It Weren't for Benjamin</u>. Human Sciences Press: New York, 1983.

Furman, B & C Beuer. Helping Kids Take Charge. In <u>Psychotherapy Networker</u>, 33(6), 65-69, Washington, DC, 2009

Gordon, T. <u>P.E.T.: Parent Effectiveness Training</u>. New American Library: New York, 1975.

Ilg, F, L. Bates & S. Baker. <u>Childhood Behavior—from the Gesell Institute of Human Development.</u> Harper Perennial: NY, 1992.

Jeddi, E. Contact comfort and behavioral thermoregulation. Physiology and Behavior. *Vol. 5(12),* December, 1970.

Kohlberg, L. Child Psychology and Childhood Education—A Cognitive-Developmental View. Longman Publishing: NY, 1987.

Moore, S. & D. Rosenthal. Sexuality in Adolescence: Current Trends. Routledge: NY, 2006.

Morely, P. M. Two-Part Harmony. Thomas Nelson, Inc.: NY, 1994.

Rogers, C. Client-Centered Therapy. Houghton Mifflin: Boston, MA, 1951.

Wright, H. N. Quiet Times for Couples. Harvest House: Eugene, OR, 1990.

Selected Readings

For additional readings on parenting, child development, relationship, and communication, the following selected readings may prove helpful.

On Parenting and Child Care

Benaroch, R. The Teen Brain. In WebMD the Magazine, New York, NY, May, 2011.

Bowen, R. Innovative Strategies for Unlocking Difficult Adolescents, Grades 7-12. Youthlight: Chapin, SC, 1998.

Bowen, R. Innovative Strategies for Unlocking Difficult Children, Grades K-6. Youthlight: Chapin, SC, 1998.

Carr, T. 131 Creative Strategies for Reaching Children with Anger Problems. Educational Media Corporation: Minneapolis, MN, 2004.

Cline, F. & J. Fay. Parenting Teens with Love and Logic (Updated and Expanded Edition). Pinon Press: Colorado Springs, CO, 2006.

Conner, B. Everyday Opportunities for Extraordinary Parenting: Simple Ways to Make a Difference in Your Child's Life-Revised Edition. Sourcebooks, Inc.: New York, NY, 2000.

Davis, C. <u>Children and the Christian Faith</u>. Broadman Press: Nashville, TN, 1979.

Dobson, J. <u>The New Dare to Discipline</u>. Tyndale House Publishers: Wheaton, IL, 2007.

Dobson, J. <u>The New Strong-Willed Child</u>. Tyndale House Publishers: Wheaton, IL, 2007.

Dobson, J. <u>Preparing for Adolescence</u>. Tyndale House Publishers: Wheaton, IL, 1978.

Dodson, F. <u>How to Discipline with Love</u>. New American Library: New York, NY, 1978.

Dodson, F. <u>How to Parent</u>. New American Library: New York, NY, 1970.

Elder, C. <u>Values and Moral Development in Children</u>. Broadman Press: Nashville, TN, 1976.

Elkind, D. <u>The Hurried Child—Growing Up Too Fast Too Soon, 25th edition</u>. DaCapp Press, Perseus Publishing Group: Cambridge, MA, 2007.

Erikson, E. <u>The Life Cycle Completed</u>. WW Norton & Co: New York, NY, 1998.

Ezzo, G. & A. M. Ezzo. <u>Growing Kids God's Way.</u> Biblical Ethics of Parenting, 4th Edition, 2007.

Fall, J. <u>Successful Parenting God's Way</u>. Thomas Nelson, Inc.: NY, 2007.

Fay, J & C Fay. <u>Love and Logic Magic for Early Childhood: Practical Parenting from Birth to</u> Six Years. Love & Logic Press: Boulder, CO, 2002.

Fay, J & F. Cline. <u>Discipline with Love and Logic Resource Guide</u>. Love & Logic Press: Boulder, CO, 2001.

Furman, B & C Beuer. Helping Kids Take Charge, in <u>Psychotherapy Networker</u> (Vol. 33, No 6)

Ginnott, H. <u>Between Parent and Child</u>. McMillan Co: NY, 1965.

Hendrick, W. <u>A Theology for Children</u>. Broadman Press: Nashville, TN, 1980.

Holloway, I. <u>To Teach A Child</u>. Broadman Press: Nashville, TN, 1979.

Kennedy, R. <u>The Encouraging Parent: How to Stop Yelling at your Kids and Start Teaching Them Confidence, Self-Discipline, and Joy</u>. Three Rivers Press, Crown Publishing Group, New York, NY, 2001.

Kimmel, T. Grace-Based Parenting. W Publishing Group, Thomas Nelson, Nashville, TN. 2004.

Kimmel, T. Grace as a Family System. In Christian Counseling Today, Vol. 18 (2), 13-15, Forest, VA, 2011.

Kimmel, T. Raising Kids Who Turn Out Right. Family Matters, 2004.

Martin, G & J. Pear. Behavior Modification-What It Is and How to Do It, 8th Edition. Prentice-Hall: NY, 2006.

Miksovsky, J. A Simple Way to Keep Your Family Humming. In USA Weekend Magazine, New York, NY, Jan 21-23, 2011.

Reisser, P, & J. Dobson. Baby & Child Care. Tyndale House Publishers: Wheaton, IL, 2007.

Schaefer, C. & T. DiGeronimo. Ages & Stages - A Parent's Guide to Normal Childhood Development. Wiley: NY, 2000.

Schmitz, C & E. Building a Love that Lasts: The Seven Surprising Secrets of Successful Marriage. Jossey-Bass Publishers: San Francisco, CA, 2008.

Tripp, T. Shepherding A Child's Heart. Shepherd Press: Wapwalloper, PA. 1995.

On Relationship and Communication

Gootnick, I. Why You Behave in Ways You Hate, and What You Can Do About It. Penmarin Books: Roseville, CA, 2000.

Levinson, D. The Seasons of A Man's Life. Ballantine Books: NY, 1986.

Perlman, H. Relationship: The Heart of Helping People. University of Chicago Press: Chicago, IL, 1979.

Price, M. Understanding Today's Children. Convention Press: Nashville, TN, 1982.

Sheehy, G. New Passages. Ballantine Books: NY. 1996.

Waldrip, S. Understanding Today's Pre-Schoolers. Convention Press: Nashville, TN, 1982.

Wicks, R. Helping Others: Ways of Listening, Sharing, and Counseling. Chilton Book Co: Radnor, PA, 1979.

Wood, J. How Do You Feel? A Guide to your Emotions. Prentice-Hall, Inc.: Englewood Cliffs, NJ, 1974.

Answers
Learning The Concept

Exercise 1: Types of Communication

1. Direct Communication
2. Checking In
3. Instructional Communication
4. Teachable Moment
5. Direct Communication
6. Instructional Communication
7. Checking In
8. Instructional Communication
9. Teachable Moment
10. Instructional Communication
11. Direct Communication
12. Checking In
13. Instructional Communication
14. Teachable Moment
15. Instructional Communication
16. Checking In
17. Teachable Moment
18. Instructional Communication
19. Teachable Moment
20. Direct Communication

Exercise 2: Verbal and Nonverbal Communication What Does It Mean?

1. J, Verbal , Clear
2. I, Nonverbal, Clear
3. O, Nonverbal, Clear
11. L, Both, Clear
12. D, Both, Mixed
13. E, Nonverbal, Clear

4. N, Nonverbal, Clear

5. M, Verbal, Mixed

6. B, Nonverbal, Mixed

7. F, Nonverbal, Clear

8. A, Both, Mixed

9. C, Both, Mixed

10. G, Both, Clear

14. H, Both, Clear

15. K, Nonverbal, Clear

16. S, Nonverbal, Clear

17. T, Both, Clear

18. Q, Verbal, Clear

19. R, Verbal, Clear

20. P, Both, Mixed

Exercise 3: Feeling Words and Sharing Feelings
Review Appendix II

Exercise 4: Active Listening and its Variations

1. Parroting

2. Active Listening

3. Noncommittal Response

4. Paraphrasing

5. Active Listening

6. Noncommittal Response

7. Noncommittal Response

8. Active Listening

9. Paraphrasing

10. Noncommittal Response

11. Active Listening

12. Paraphrasing

13. Parroting

14. Active Listening

15. Paraphrasing

16. Noncommittal Response

17. Paraphrasing

18. Active Listening

19. Active Listening

20. Noncommittal Response

21. Noncommittal Response

22. Active Listening

23. Parroting

24. Noncommittal Response

25. Paraphrasing

Exercise 5: Earned Authority vs. Ascribed Authority

1. Earned Authority

2. Earned Authority

3. Ascribed Authority

4. Earned Authority

5. Ascribed Authority

6. Earned Authority

11. Ascribed Authority

12. Ascribed Authority

13. Earned Authority

14. Ascribed Authority

15. Ascribed Authority

16. Earned Authority

7. Ascribed Authority

8. Ascribed Authority

9. Earned Authority

10. Ascribed Authority

17. Ascribed Authority

18. Earned Authority

19. Earned Authority

20. Ascribed Authority

Exercise 6: Servanthood Parenting

1. Doormat

2. Doormat

3. Servanthood Parenting

4. Doormat

5. Servanthood Parenting

6. Servanthood Parenting

7. Doormat

8. Servanthood Parenting

9. Servanthood Parenting

10. Doormat

11. Servanthood Parenting

12. Servanthood Parenting

13. Doormat

14. Doormat

15. Servanthood Parenting

Exercise 7: Developmental Stages of Parenting

1. Advice-Based

2. Directed

3. Hands On

4. Directed

5. Hands On

6. Consultative

7. Directed

8. Advice-Based

9. Consultative

10. Hands On

11. Directed

12. Advice-Based

13. Advice-Based

14. Consultative

Exercise 8: Defining Roles and Expectations

Take time to write down family job descriptions and expectations, and to assign roles.

Exercise 9: Boundaries and Choices

1. Boundary

2. Boundary

3. Boundary

4. Boundary

9. Choice

10. Boundary

11. Choice

12. Choice

5. Choice	13. Choice
6. Choice	14. Boundary
7. Choice	15. Boundary
8. Choice	

Exercise 10: Boundaries Exercise—Family Rules

Use the space provided on pages 54 to list your brainstormed family rules and job descriptions. Then transfer them to a sheet of paper to post on your family communication board.

Exercise 11: Punishment vs. Natural Consequences

1. Punishment	9. Punishment
2. Punishment	10. Natural Consequence
3. Natural Consequence	11. Natural Consequence
4. Natural Consequence	12. Punishment
5. Punishment	13. Natural Consequence
6. Natural Consequences	14. Punishment
7. Natural Consequence	15. Punishment
8. Natural Consequence	

Exercise 12: Developmental Ages and Stages

On the space allowed on pages 69-72, brainstorm and list behaviors children demonstrate at the various ages and stages.

Exercise 13: Know the Language—Decoding Words and Actions

I'm not interested or don't want to talk.

Hi! I get it.

Laugh Out Loud

I'm supposed to say something, but don't know what to say, or, I'm off in space.

I don't know.

I'm not going there.

I'll be late.

I want to know and understand what you are saying.

That's a surprise.

I'm not interested.

I understand and want to connect with you.

I'm too cool to be seen with you.

I completely agree.

I'm into this completely.

What are you going to do about it?

Exercise 14: Benevolent Despotism

In the space provided, answer the questions.

Exercise 15: Re Charging Your Batteries Daily

In the space provided, fill in the blanks to complete the contract with yourself.

Exercise 16: The Contest for Re-Energizing

In the space provided, answer the questions and distinguish self-care from other-care.

Exercise 17: The Emotional Side of Hormones

In the space provided, complete the lists of physical and emotional changes for boys and girls, as they go through puberty.

Exercise 18: Diet and Activity

Review Appendix 6 to see how this might be of help to you or your family.

Exercise 19: Confidante Relationship

Who is your confidante? What makes that person so?

Exercise 20: Personal Journaling

Review Appendix 7 to see how this might benefit you.

Exercise 21: Telling Your Stories

Write down your stories of teenage rebellion and share them in a family meeting.

Exercise 22: Restrictions That Work

In the space provided, take time to compare the relational and correctional models of restriction.

Exercise 23: Catch Them Being Good

Sweetheart, you are getting to be such a big boy, using your knife to cut your meat. (POSITIVE) But you know what? If you hold it this way (demonstrate) it will cut better. (NEGATIVE) Give it a try. I know you'll get it soon. (POSITIVE)

Aww, man! Son you are getting some serious studying in tonight. (POSITIVE) I just don't think it's a good idea to keep the iPod cranked up and dance around your room if you plan to ace that test tomorrow. Turn off the music for just another twenty minutes, and I will come in to quiz you on what you've studied. (NEGATIVE) Gosh, some day you're gonna make me a rich man with your music, ya know? (POSITIVE)

Wow! Teaching you to drive, hon, is a breeze. You've got almost all of the rules of the road down pat. (POSITIVE) We need to get some more drive time in so you can practice what you know. (NEGATIVE) Before long you will be driving like a champ. (POSITIVE)

Now, take time to create three catch-them-being-good sequences with your children from your life.

Exercise 24: Changing What if's Into I wonders

What if...?	I wonder...
1. What if they tease me about being a girl and trying out for the baseball team?	1. I wonder how well I will be able to ignore their teasing & have a good tryout?
2. What if I'm not good enough to make the team?	2. I wonder how well my tryout will go?

3. What if I goof up and can't do it right?

3. I wonder how well I will bounce back from any mistakes I might make?

4. What if they don't like me?

4. I wonder how many friends I will make today?

5. What if I don't know anybody trying out?

5. I wonder who I will approach and talk to today?

Exercise 25: Responsible Freedom
Take a moment to put into your own words what the Principle of Responsible Freedom means to you. Talk to your spouse/family about how you can apply this concept in your family life? How will it make your lives go more smoothly?

Exercise 26: The Rules
After discussion with your spouse/family, use the space provided to write down the ten most fundamental rules by which you want your home to function.

Exercise 27: Accountability and Oversight
In the space provided, list ways in which you do, or would like to, provide accountability and oversight for your teens activities.